RICE
IS
LIFE

RICE IS LIFE

Recipes and Stories
Celebrating the World's
Most Essential Grain

CARYL LEVINE + KEN LEE
of LOTUS FOODS
with KRISTIN DONNELLY
Recipe Photographs by ERIN SCOTT

CHRONICLE BOOKS
SAN FRANCISCO

Library of Congress Cataloging-in-Publication Data available.

ISBN 978-1-7972-1490-0

Manufactured in China.

Food styling by Lillian Kang.
Food styling assistance by Paige Arnett and Huxly McCorkle.
Photo and prop assistance by Eliza Miller.
Design by Lizzie Vaughan.
Typesetting by Katy Brown.
Typeset in Mark and Mabry Mono.

All photographs by Erin Scott except as indicated below.

Other Image Credits
Pages 2–3, 19, 65 (bottom), 120 (bottom), 159 (top right and bottom), 234–35: Photographs copyright © Erika Styger. Pages 6–7, 15, 58, 59 (top left), 120 (top left and top right), 121 (top and bottom right), 159 (top left), 227, 248–49: Photographs copyright © Sue Price. Page 18: Photo by mbrand85, used under license from Shutterstock.com. Page 20 (top left): Photograph copyright © Sabarmatee. Page 20 (bottom): Photograph copyright © Sahaja Samrudha/India. Page 20 (top right): Photograph by frank60, used under license from Shutterstock.com. Page 23, 256: Photographs copyright © Rosemary Glos. Page 30: Photograph by wattana, used under license from Shutterstock.com. Page 34: Photograph by Andrea Cherchi, used under license from Shutterstock.com. Page 59 (top right): Photograph copyright © Sato Shuichi. Page 59 (bottom): Photograph copyright © Caryl Levine. Page 65 (top): Photograph by Sushantanet, used under license from Shutterstock.com. Page 82: Photographs courtesy of SRI-Rice. Page 85, 121 (bottom left), 158, 219, 244 (top left and bottom): Photographs by Vong Savoeun, provided courtesy of Lotus Foods. Page 91: Photograph by Mangporbinvon, used under license from Shutterstock. com. Page 160–61: Photograph by Arthur Teng, used under license from Shutterstock.com. Page 201: Photograph courtesy of Foodtech Solutions (Thailand) Co., Ltd. Page 247: Photograph by sutlafk, used under license from Shutterstock.com. Back cover image: Photograph by yankane, used under license from Shutterstock.com.

10 9 8 7 6 5 4 3 2 1

Chronicle books and gifts are available at special quantity discounts to corporations, professional associations, literacy programs, and other organizations. For details and discount information, please contact our premiums department at corporatesales@chroniclebooks.com or at 1-800-759-0190.

Chronicle Books LLC
680 Second Street
San Francisco, California 94107
www.chroniclebooks.com

CONTENTS

4

MAIN DISHES

5

DESSERTS

INTRODUCTION

This book was more than twenty-five years in the making—a love story of sorts, about the incredible diversity of a common grain that sustains half the world's people. It's our ode to the nuanced and distinct flavors of heirloom varieties and the innovative methods by which they can be grown to reduce damaging environmental impacts and empower the lives of those who grow them. And, of course, it's a celebration of the infinite ways this humble, gluten-free pantry staple can be transformed into the most flavorful and nourishing dishes. Here's to rice, the world's most essential grain.

Our story with rice begins in a small Dai village in China's southern Yunnan Province, on the border of Laos and Myanmar. We don't remember our exact meal in the thatch-roofed restaurant that night long ago, but we do remember the rice. Grains the color of the midnight sky, overwhelmingly fragrant and the star of the meal. The day after we tried the unforgettable black rice, we headed straight to the market looking for anyone who could tell us more about it. We learned it was an heirloom variety called longevity rice, because of its nutritional value, or tribute rice, because according to legend, it was reserved for the emperors to ensure their good health.

At home in the United States, we had only ever seen white and brown rice. Black rice, for us, was something new. It was 1993, and we—Caryl Levine and Ken Lee—were a young couple seeking our next adventure and purpose. China had opened up to more foreign trade and investment, and we sensed opportunity. What from America could we bring to China? We saved our pennies and took leaves of absence from our jobs so we could find out. As we continued traveling through this immense and captivating country, we noticed more black rice at the local markets, but we rarely saw people eating it. Culturally, most people in China preferred white rice as the staple in their daily meals, and they reserved black rice as a medicinal ingredient, prescribed by doctors as a blood tonifier and to help people regain their strength. During a tour of the Forbidden City, the home of the emperors, Ken thought that the name *Forbidden Rice* had an intriguing ring to it. Instead of bringing something from the United States to China, we thought, how about importing black rice from China to the US?

Before returning from our two-month trip, we shipped 4 lb [1.8 kg] of black rice to our home in the Bay Area of California, one of the most forward-thinking and innovative food hubs in the country at the time. With newly arrived samples in hand, Ken knocked on the kitchen doors of local chefs including Gary Danko, Alice Waters, and Roland Passot, offering a taste of the forbidden! Almost everyone called us and asked, "How can I get it?" This little bit of market research confirmed our instincts: This rice is spectacular, and we need to bring it here. The question was, *how?*

In 1994, we trademarked *Forbidden Rice* to differentiate it from other black rice varieties, and it took us two long years to figure out how to import it. It turned out what we had nicknamed Forbidden Rice was forbidden to us. At the time, most companies in China involved in international trade were large or government controlled. We struggled to find someone willing to take a chance on us and send us a mere pallet of rice. Eventually, we met a young couple, Zuojin Wang and Long Rong, who, like us, were eager to take advantage of China's opening to private enterprise. Zuojin was an engineer working in a large company in Northern China, while Long previously had a successful business exporting seafood. They told us they'd be happy to work directly with farmers who grew black rice in

China's sub-arctic Heilongjiang Province, the geographical limit of where rice can be grown.

The black rice there is a long-season, cold-tolerant variety, very different from most black rice that is grown in tropical regions. *Heilongjiang* means "Black Dragon River," which is the Chinese name for the river Amur. The region is famous for its humus-rich, highly fertile black soils and has become China's organic grain basket. High soil fertility enhances yields without the need for synthetic fertilizer and low temperatures, which serve as a natural pesticide, thereby facilitating organic production. To this day, our black rice is grown in small batches on family-owned farms and not on a large commercial scale. Our creation of an international market for this unique ancient rice has helped keep it in production, and the families from whom we source the rice benefit from higher price premiums from Lotus Foods.

From the beginning, we committed ourselves to fair trade and organic agriculture. This wasn't just a niche for us. We believe that agriculture must wean itself from inorganic fertilizers and toxic pesticides for the health of people and our planet. We also believe that providing farmers with a sustainable livelihood is a moral imperative.

In 2005, ten years into our business, our mission became even more ambitious: We would commit to changing how rice is grown around the world. After learning about a rice-growing method called the System of Rice Intensification (read more about it on page 55), we realized that SRI could help conserve water, improve soil health, increase food security, and mitigate climate change. We committed to purchasing as much rice as possible from farmers practicing SRI and supporting efforts to expand adoption of SRI around the world.

Almost three decades since introducing our Forbidden Rice® to Bay Area chefs, we now import a variety of rices, including bamboo-infused Jade Pearl Rice™, heirloom basmati and jasmine rice, traditional brick-colored red rice, a tri-color blend, and an expanding line of organic rice-based noodle products. Each rice has its own distinctive flavor and texture that we consider when we cook. It not only brings a delicate floral flavor and intriguing color to our meals but a host of health-giving micronutrients too.

With this book, we hope to encourage you to choose your rice with as much care as you do your fresh produce, considering how it's grown and the livelihoods of the farmers who grow it. As we developed recipes for this book, we looked to the great rice cultures of the world for inspiration. Given so many varieties and endless preparation possibilities, we chose to focus on recipes where rice and rice noodles are an integral part of the dish—not just something to have alongside. We also prioritized simplicity, assuring a home cook's ability to make many of these dishes on busy weeknights. Most of the recipes include ingredients you can find at any supermarket or health food store, but a few might require a trip to an Asian market.

Some of the farming families we work with in Thailand, Indonesia, and India generously shared some of their favorite home recipes as well, which we are proud to include. While all these recipes are to enjoy as written, we also hope they inspire you to experiment and play—swap out a rice variety for one you have on hand and any vegetables that are in season. We focused on including many vegetarian and plant-based recipes. For those recipes that include animal protein, we often offer a vegetarian alternative. Most of all, we hope this book and these recipes help you more confidently cook rice and see it as an exciting meal foundation full of glorious possibilities. Happy cooking!

TOP RIGHT: The rice cycle begins. Mature rice seedlings are transported to fields for transplanting, which is largely done by women.

BOTTOM RIGHT: Seedlings are then pressed deep into flooded fields, sometimes in rows but generally at random in clumps of about 5 seedlings. The women labor bent over, with their hands and legs immersed in muddy water, which can harbor leeches, malarial mosquitos, and other disease vectors.

ON RICE

What Is Rice Anyway?

At its most elemental, rice is the edible seed of a grass plant in the genus *Oryza*, and we humans have been eating rice for a very long time. Its origins and its history as a cultivated crop remain robust areas of study, with as many questions as answers. The oldest archaeological evidence shows humans had rice in their lives as far back as 11,000 to 12,000 BCE in the Yangtze River Valley in China. Back then, it might have been foraged still and not yet deliberately planted. Archeologists have also found evidence of rice consumption in the Ganges Valley in northern India dating back to 7,000 to 5,000 BCE. It's clear that by 4,000 BCE, people cultivated rice in the lower Yangtze River Valley, and to this day, about two-thirds of China's rice is grown in the Yangtze River Basin.

In Africa, rice probably emerged in the flood basin of central Niger, and people brought it west to what is now Senegal, south to the New Guinea Coast, and east to Lake Chad. As in Asia, rice started off as a foraged food, and at least 3,500 years ago, people intentionally planted it as a crop, selecting it over time for different characteristics.

Rice now grows in many diverse types of climates on every continent except Antarctica. Wherever possible, rice is grown under irrigated conditions, but in many areas, rain-fed rice is cultivated. The two most domesticated species are *Oryza*

sativa, commonly known as Asian rice, and *Oryza glaberrima*, also known as African rice. Most commercial and subsistence rice production in the world is dominated by Asian rice cultivars. But smallholder farmers in West Africa are still growing *Oryza glaberrima* in unique environments not suitable to the Asian rice varieties. These landscape niches can include mangrove and saltwater areas, upland areas, riverbeds, and lake shores where farmers developed highly specialized cropping systems over the past 3,500 years. Although *O. glaberrima* might not reach the productivity levels of *O. sativa*, it plays a critical role in contributing to peoples' food security and livelihoods throughout West Africa.

How Does Rice Grow?

Rice grows in more diverse climates than any other crop. Depending on the variety, it can tolerate the sweltering heat and frequent rains in the tropics as well as temperate climates as

low as 40°F [4.5°C]. It is grown at a range of elevations and in diverse ecosystems, from the low-lying Mekong Delta to terraces in the Himalayan mountains, and even at the edge of the Sahara Desert in Timbuktu, Mali. In warm, humid climates, farmers can sometimes harvest two or three crops per year.

As rice grows, it looks like fields of waving green grass. As it matures, it produces tassels of seeds (the rice grains) that hang from the plant. The inedible protective sheath—known as the husk or hull—enrobing the seeds on most commercial rice ripens from green to golden in color, but other, more traditional varieties have gorgeous deep purple, brick-red, or pastel-toned husks hiding the rice inside. Rice growers separate the rice from the stalks by threshing—beating stalks by hand or mechanically— to loosen and remove the grain from its stalk.

At this point, the rice is still in its husk. To make the grains easier to remove, they are dried in the sun for several days or with a drying machine for several hours. Through friction created either

by hand in traditional rice milling or by machines in industrial processes, the husk is removed to reveal the bran layer that surrounds unmilled grains. For whole-grain rice, the bran layer is left intact. For white rice, the fiber-rich bran and nutritious germ are milled off, leaving the mostly starchy interior behind.

A Rice Rainbow: The Beauty of Biodiversity

Like heirloom beans, tomatoes, corn, and squash, rice comes in a kaleidoscope of colors. Scientists estimate there were once about 140,000 different varieties of rice cultivated around the world. Some 132,000 varieties of rice and wild relatives are currently stored in the International Rice Genebank maintained by the International Rice Research Institute in the Philippines.

Until the mid-twentieth century, farmers grew tens of thousands of different indigenous varieties of rice that had evolved and adapted to their climate and soil. The Green Revolution of the 1960s and '70s transformed global agriculture, helping to triple rice production to feed a hungry planet, but also leading to a dramatic loss of rice biodiversity by displacing traditional varieties with new "improved" modern varieties. In Thailand, experts estimate that farmers once tended to 16,000 different varieties, but by the year 2000, only some 37 varieties of rice were being widely grown. Similarly, it is reported that in India, the number of rice varieties being cultivated has decreased from roughly 100,000 to 7,000 since the 1970s. A 2017 study found that in most Asian rice-producing countries, the top three modern varieties being grown comprised at least one-third of their total rice area. Worldwide, scientists believe that between 1900 and 2000, we lost about 75 percent of the genetic diversity in major food crops and continue to lose more diversity at an annual rate of 1 to 2 percent. Why does this matter?

Only about 10 percent of the rice grown in the world today is traded on the international market. Most is consumed within the country where it is grown. As is true with heirloom vegetables, heirloom varieties of rice are open-pollinated, meaning the seeds can be saved and grown back true to form the following year. They also allow growers to select seeds from the strongest plants to help them adapt better to their own climate so that they ultimately produce more nutritious rice. Since founding Lotus Foods, we have been passionate about bringing heirloom varieties of rice to a larger market. Our interest first started because of their appealing flavors and colors, and then we soon learned about the benefits of preserving rice biodiversity for the people and the planet.

Scientists develop most modern commercial varieties with little consideration for tradition and nutrition, instead focusing on producing seeds with high yields that require the use of chemical fertilizers, pesticides, and herbicides to grow well. This means that once farmers move away from their traditional varieties to these modern varieties, they often must purchase new seeds year after year as well as inputs like chemical fertilizers, herbicides, and pesticides, leaving them dependent on dealers and often in debt. A key strategy to improve biodiversity is to encourage farmers to continue growing diverse varieties of rice on their farms.

Modern varieties can contain fewer micronutrients than traditional varieties, potentially diminishing the health of the people who rely on rice as their main food source. There's also a cultural loss for younger generations who don't know or remember the rice of previous generations, which was often more flavorful and nutritious than the rice grown today, and sometimes had medicinal and spiritual significance. Finally, farmers who grow multiple traditional varieties of rice are better positioned to deal with unpredictable weather patterns due to climate change. If one variety in their fields fails, hopefully the others will not.

At Lotus Foods, we're proud to help create a market for heirloom rice, because it encourages farmers to continue growing these healthier traditional varieties for themselves to eat and sell. We also champion efforts around the world to salvage and revive lost varieties. By purchasing heirloom rice, you are helping preserve a piece of history and culture and contributing to a better world.

The Two Categories of Rice

Some people think rice must be long-grain, fluffy, and separate, while others think it should be shorter and stickier. The truth is, there isn't only one type of rice. Your favorite style of rice might just depend on the variety of rice you're used to eating or your cooking preferences, which can vary by culture or even by family.

O. sativa is divided into two categories: japonica and indica. Japonica is generally grown in more temperate climates and the grains are shorter and rounder. It contains more amylopectin, a sticky type of starch that makes the grains cling together when cooked. Javanica is a sub-variety of japonica that grows in tropical climates and has medium-size grains that are also a bit sticky.

Indica is often found in tropical and warm subtropical climates and tends to have longer grains and more amylose, a dry starch that makes the rice fluffy with separate grains when cooked.

Grain Size and Color

At the store, you'll often find rice classified as short-grain, medium-grain, and long-grain. In general, long-grain rice varieties are four to five times as long as they are wide, while medium-grain varieties are two to three times longer than the width of the grains. Short-grain rice has nearly the same width as the length, and the grains tend to cling together when cooked.

No matter the grain size, rice can be milled so it's white. Otherwise, it can be hulled and left as a whole grain or partially milled so some of the bran layer is intact. White rice is completely devoid of the nutritious bran layer and germ. It's prized for its gentle sweetness, softness, and pearly grains. Without the oil-containing germ, it has a longer shelf life and faster cooking time. White rice grown in the United States is enriched with some of the vitamins and minerals removed during the milling process. Whole-grain rice is most often known as brown rice, and most of what you'll see on the shelves is tan in color. Whole-grain rice varieties have the bran and germ intact and can be black or red as well. Their flavors are more prominent, earthy, and robust, and the textures are heartier.

Much of the rice sold is not distinguished beyond its grain size and color. Unless they are labeled otherwise, they are not aromatic varieties, meaning their flavors and aromas are very subtle. The list of rice on the following pages is not exhaustive but includes many of the styles and varieties you might encounter at the store or through specialty purveyors in the United States.

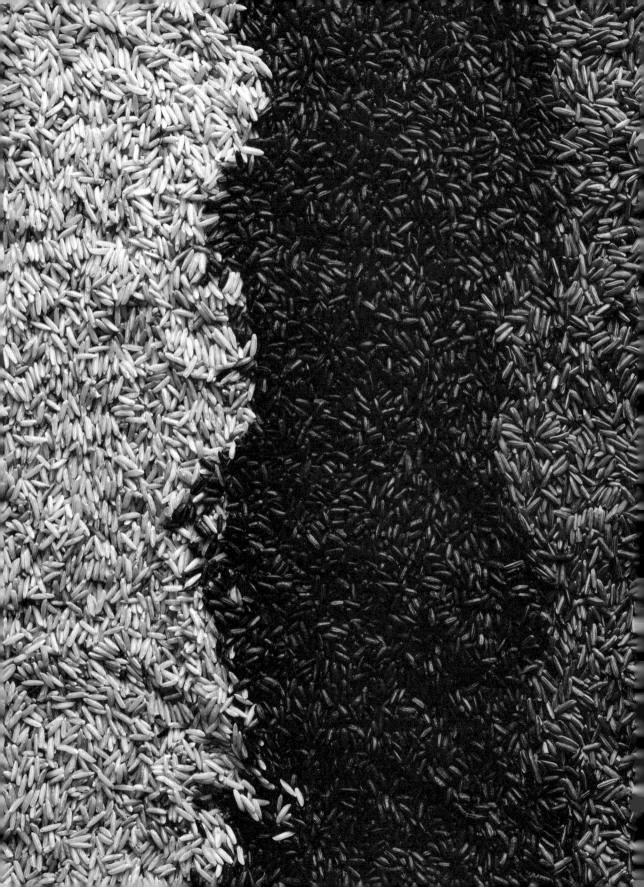

RICE VARIETIES FROM AROUND THE WORLD

East and Southeast Asian Varieties

The oldest archaeological evidence of rice use by humans has been found in the middle and lower Yangtze River Valley region of China. Most of the people living in East and Southeast Asia rely on rice for daily sustenance. Milled white rice is the most popular, but you will see whole-grain black rice and red rice sold for medicinal purposes or as a specialty food. While we associate these varieties with this part of the world, many of them now grow in other countries, including the United States.

BLACK RICE

The black or purple pigment in black rice comes from plant compounds known as anthocyanins, which are frequently touted for their antioxidant properties. These are the same compounds that give blueberries and purple cabbage their color. Researchers recently found that the mutation of a specific gene stimulates the production of the black pigment. You can find black rice varieties of all kinds, whether indica or japonica, in pockets of production throughout Asia. People have traditionally prized them for their rareness and supposed medicinal properties. As a natural source of anthocyanins, black rice has a myriad of health benefits, including possible anti-cancer properties. It has three times as much iron as brown rice, which might be why Chinese doctors prescribe it as a blood tonifier and kidney tonic. Black rice varieties are now being grown outside Asia, including in the United States, Italy, and Brazil. Thanks to the prevalence of Thai restaurants, many Americans have tasted black sticky rice, which is a bit sweet and often used in desserts.

In 1994, we trademarked the name *Forbidden Rice®* to differentiate the non-sticky heirloom variety we import and its growing environment. When cooked, the shiny onyx grains turn deep purple, cling together slightly, and have a subtle floral aroma.

JASMINE RICE

Jasmine rice is a fragrant medium- to long-grain variety that originated in Thailand and Cambodia but is now grown around the world. It's one of the rice varieties of choice in much of Southeast Asia and parts of China. In Thailand, the premier jasmine is called Thai Hom Mali; in Cambodia, the equivalent is Phka Malis, which in the Khmer language means "beautiful garland of flowers" because of the rice's delicate floral aroma. Thai Hom Mali and Phka Malis consistently come out on top as the World's Best Rice in an annual global competition, though in 2015 they were edged out by California's Calrose! In our early days, we distributed the first organic American-grown jasmine rice based on Thai seed stock. We now import the premium variety of both milled white and whole-grain brown jasmine rice from Thailand and Cambodia.

RED RICE

Red rice varieties have a ruddy-toned bran layer, and they can be aromatic as well as nonaromatic. Historically, red rice was prevalent in almost all rice-growing countries of Asia, appreciated for its taste, texture, and health benefits. In India, Ayurvedic physicians used these varieties as medicine for centuries. These locally evolved varieties adapted well to many different environments with tolerance for infertile soils, deep water, and drought, and resistance to pests and diseases. With the advent of the Green Revolution and emphasis on breeding new high-yielding varieties of white rice, thousands of traditional red rice varieties disappeared; if they showed up in the fields, they were thought of as weeds. Bhutanese red rice, a traditional variety grown high in the Himalayas, was the very first rice we ever distributed. We now import red jasmine rice with a bran layer that's the color of brick from Southeast Asia. Red rice has a rich, nutty flavor and toothsome texture. Today, many countries grow varieties of red rice, including the United States. In 2018, Cornell University and the US Department of Agriculture announced the launch of the first red rice to be released for production in the United States, called Scarlett.

RICEBERRY

A relative newcomer to the market, Riceberry (also marketed as Jasberry) was developed by researchers in Thailand with the aim of combining the nutritional value of black rice with the taste and fragrance of jasmine. It has a purple pigment and the texture of brown rice when cooked but is softer and fluffier on the inside.

STICKY RICE

Also known as sweet rice and glutinous rice (not to be confused with gluten, as it contains none), these varieties contain no amylose, so they are exceptionally and appealingly sticky. You can find every color of sticky rice, from white to brown to purple to red, but the white is most common; pigmented sticky rice is often reserved for holidays or special occasions. While sticky rice is used in some savory dishes, it is also a common ingredient in desserts. In some countries, around Lunar New Year, you'll find cakes of the cooked rice, sometimes wrapped in leaves. To prevent sticky rice from becoming mushy, it is often steamed. The rice is also ground to make a glutinous (or sweet rice) flour that produces a stretchy dough. For example, the delightfully chewy exteriors of Japanese mochi ice cream cakes are made with a glutinous rice dough.

SHORT-GRAIN RICE

Sometimes sold in the United States as sushi rice, this is a popular style of rice in Japan and Korea. When rinsed and cooked properly, the grains take on a pearly sheen and stick together while retaining a sense of separateness. Short-grain rice can be either white or brown. Koshihikari is a famous cultivar of this rice beloved for its delicacy and is grown in Japan, California, and Australia. Akitakomachi is grown in the Akita prefecture of Japan and is known for its especially small and glossy grains.

South Asian Varieties

There are thousands of varieties of rice throughout South Asia, and we only see a few of them in the United States. Northern India's beloved basmati rice is the most well-known South Asian variety, and it's the most widely exported. Cultivars of it now grow all over the world.

BASMATI

The word *basmati* comes from the Sanskrit word *vasmati*, meaning "fragrant." High in the dry starch amylose, the long, slender grains become fluffy and separate when cooked in dishes like pulaos and biryani from the Indian subcontinent. Since Iranian rice is hard to find in the United States, it is also frequently used here in Persian rice dishes. Many cooks prize aged basmati, which is slightly yellow in hue, because it produces drier, fluffier rice when cooked. Most basmati is now grown from hybrid seeds bred for yields, not taste. The basmati rice we import is an heirloom variety known as Dehraduni, which is sometimes referred to as the "mother of all basmati." It has a gorgeous floral fragrance. Through a unique partnership with organic farmers in northern India who are using the System of Rice Intensification (see page 55 for more), our basmati became the first Regenerative Organic Certified (ROC) rice—preserving this heirloom rice for generations to come.

IDLI RICE

This polished, pearly, medium-grain rice is popular in southern India and Sri Lanka for soaking and cooking to turn into idli cakes, a common breakfast dish in that part of the world.

KALIJIRA

Considered the premium rice of choice in Bengal, Kalijira is known as the Prince of Rice or baby basmati because of its delicious and delicate flavor. In the US, you will sometimes see bags of Kalijira also mislabeled as Govindabhog rice, which is a similarly sized but distinctive variety that grows in some of the same regions. This tiny aromatic rice cooks in only 10 minutes, producing firm yet tender separate grains. Although in Bengal (today comprised of the Indian state of West Bengal and Bangladesh) it is traditionally used for special occasions and religious ceremonies (as is Govindabhog), it can be enjoyed as an everyday steamed rice or as an alternative to basmati. We now offer Kalijira rice as Quick Cook Rice.

RED BASMATI

Sometimes known as Sri Lankan red rice, this long-grain variety has a red hull that cooks up fluffy and separate, like basmati.

SONA MASOORI

Aromatic with a medium grain, this rice is mostly cultivated in Southern India.

African Varieties

As the fastest-emerging cereal crop in sub-Saharan Africa and the second major source of calories on the continent, rice is one of Africa's most important crops. *O. glaberrima* is unique to Africa and was domesticated in West Africa about 3,000 years ago, but has been part of the diaspora of African plants to the "New World." Presently, it is not traded internationally. Compared to *O. sativa*, *O. glaberrima* is characterized by its red and black hulls and smaller size. After traders from India introduced *O. sativa* to East Africa in the early 1500s, Asian rice varieties spread westward. Today, Asian varieties, and especially basmati, prevail across the continent, and cultivation of *O. glaberrima* has declined. Very little of the rice grown in Africa is exported outside the continent, and it's rare to find African-grown rice in the United States. In Suriname, the Saamaka, descendants of enslaved people brought to Latin America from West Africa, still cultivate both species in the same field (see page 23).

OFADA RICE

Named for Ofada, a town in the Ogun state in southwest Nigeria where it is largely grown, this rice is generally a mix that can include indigenous African varieties as well as Asian varieties. It is whole-grain rice that is traditionally soaked and fermented before drying, a process that gives the rice its distinctive taste. It is often served alongside stews.

RED BEARDED UPLAND RICE

This heirloom rice from West Africa dates back to at least the nineteenth century and likely earlier. It has been preserved since then in Trinidad by the descendants of Merikens, Africans who settled there after gaining freedom from enslavement by serving in the War of 1812, as well as Indigenous people. The Merikens likely brought this rice variety with them from the American South. The grain has a rust-colored bran layer, which is how it got its name. In Trinidad, the rice goes by the name Moruga Hill Rice, named after where it is grown.

You can purchase Moruga Hill rice from Trinidad in specialty markets and online. While not yet widely cultivated in the United States, it could be soon. This variety has excited many African American chefs because it further links them to their history as well as the rice cooking of their ancestors.

European Varieties

Historians speculate that rice was introduced to Greece after Alexander the Great's expedition to India in 326 BCE. The Romans knew rice only as an extremely expensive commodity imported in small quantities from India for medicinal purposes. Rice cultivation began in Egypt in the seventh century, and the Arabs then introduced rice production to the Iberian Peninsula (today Portugal and Spain) at the time of its conquest in 711 CE. By the mid-fifteenth century, rice was being cultivated in Italy and then France. Today, rice cultivation happens in pockets of the continent, and the varieties are used to produce iconic dishes like risotto and paella. Some of these varieties, like arborio, have moved with migration and are cultivated more widely, while others have stayed mostly local and are sold in the United States as specialty imports.

ARBORIO

This popular Italian variety is now grown in the United States and Argentina, and it is commonly used to make risotto. Its oval-shaped, medium-size grains are incredibly starchy—perfect for thickening liquid into a creamy-seeming sauce. While brown arborio rice does exist, it does not release its starch the same way.

BALDO

Like arborio, baldo rice can absorb a lot of liquid and is typically used to make Turkish pilafs.

BOMBA

This medium-grain rice is one of the rice varieties from Spain used to make paella. It's known for absorbing a lot of liquid while remaining pleasantly al dente with separate grains. When grown near Valencia, Spain, it is one of the varieties that can be known as Valencia rice.

CALASPARRA

Another Spanish rice used to make paella, this rice has a protected Denominación de Origen, which means it must be from in and around the town of Calasparra to be called by this name. You can buy white Calasparra rice when it's white or "semi-brown," which means it is partially polished to retain more of its nutrition.

CAMARGUE

Rice production began between the fifteenth and sixteenth centuries in the Camargue region of southern France. After World War II, money from the Marshall Plan (aimed at revitalizing Europe) was invested in the area, which allowed irrigation and drainage ditches to be created. This turned marshy land in the Camargue region into rice-growing country. While farmers there grow a few different varieties, the region has become most well-known for its red rice. By

2000, the Riz de Camargue had obtained the European Protected Geographical Indication label. The grains of this "riz rouge" tend to be medium-grain and firm with some stickiness.

CARNAROLI
From northern Italy, this rice is often called the King of Italian rice or the caviar of rice. It has a higher starch content and firmer texture than arborio, so some cooks think it makes the best risotto. It's mostly grown in northern Italy, with some production in Argentina.

VENERE
A recently developed hybrid of a Chinese black rice and an Italian rice, Venere rice is a medium-grain rice with a dark black color, a sweet nutty taste, and an aroma reminiscent of freshly baked bread. It is grown in Piedmont and Sardinia and means "Venus rice" in Italian.

VIALONE NANO
The risotto rice of choice in Venice, Vialone Nano is beloved for its fat, short grains that absorb at least twice their weight in liquid while retaining their shape. Grown in northeastern Italy since 1937, it is a cross between Vialone rice and a short-statured variety called Nano. In 1996, Veronese Vialone Nano rice was given the protected geographical indication (Italian: IGP), under the name of Riso Nano Vialone Veronese IGP. You can find this rice from specialty purveyors.

American Varieties

In North America, indigenous rice from the *Zizania* genus—often called wild rice—grows naturally in lakes and streams in the Great Lakes region of the United States and Canada. Since the 1960s, the species has also been cultivated in flooded paddies, mostly in California. The true wild grain is a vital and sacred food for Indigenous people who live around the Great Lakes. Traditionally, the deep-brown, slender grains are hand-harvested in canoes and dried over an open fire, resulting in grains with a soft texture and sweet, lightly smoky flavor. Commercial "wild" rice, sometimes called paddy rice, is chewier, blander, and often blended with other rice varieties to add texture. In this book, we focus exclusively on *O. sativa*, but we wanted to mention this important indigenous grain here.

Spanish and Portuguese colonizers introduced *Oryza* rice to the Americas, and the Portuguese brought enslaved Africans to work on its cultivation in Brazil in the 1500s, thus beginning the tumultuous history of rice in the "New World." In the 1700s, slave traders brought West Africans skilled in rice cultivation to South Carolina and Georgia; enslaved people created unbelievable and undeserved wealth for landowners in this area before the Civil War. In other parts of the marshy South, farmers grew rice for sustenance, and many now grow it commercially in Arkansas, Texas, Mississippi, and Louisiana.

When Chinese laborers moved to California for the Gold Rush, the birth of the California rice industry soon followed, and the state now grows many varieties of rice at huge industrial scales. The United States exports about half the rice it grows.

In South America, rice is an increasingly important cereal crop, grown by both small-scale subsistence farmers and industrial growers. Cooks there tend to prefer medium- to long-grain nonaromatic white rice. Several countries in South America also export rice, but they are not usually sold as distinctive varieties. The popularity of many rice dishes throughout the Americas and the Caribbean shows the long-lasting influence of African and Asian cooking on North and South American food.

CALROSE

A high-yielding, medium-grain rice grown throughout California, this Japanese-style rice is the founding variety of the modern California rice industry. Released in 1948, it comprises most of California's annual rice crop. Calrose rice grains are soft and stick together, making it good for use in sushi.

CAROLINA GOLD RICE

No one knows for sure how this variety came to what is now the United States, but on the eve of the American Revolution, the long, elegant grains of Carolina Gold Rice made the Lowcountry—the coastal area of South Carolina and Georgia—the wealthiest area in North America. Yet this wealth was derived directly from the labor and expert knowledge of rice cultivation of enslaved West Africans, especially women. The Civil War and a major hurricane in 1911 ended the rice plantation culture and technology of the Carolina Lowcountry, although descendants of enslaved Africans—known as Gullah Geechee—continued to cultivate rice for home use until about the 1960s. An eye surgeon in Savannah named Richard Schulze found the seeds for Carolina Gold in a USDA seed bank in the mid-1980s and started growing it as a hobby—believe it or not, to attract ducks to his land for hunting. He eventually grew enough Carolina Gold Rice to sell, and it's now grown by other farmers and sold by small mills like Anson Mills. Cooks then as now prize this rice because of its clean flavor and versatility—it works well when cooked as distinct, separate grains or as risotto.

CHARLESTON GOLD

An offspring of Carolina Gold and a lost variety called Charleston Long, this rice is new to the scene and was developed by breeders in 2005. Unlike Carolina Gold, this variety is highly aromatic, more like basmati.

KOKUHO ROSE

Developed for the California company Koda Farms in 1963, this rice is a cross between Calrose and a Middle Eastern rice and is prized for its sweeter flavor.

Founder of Koda Farms Keisaburo Koda started farming rice in California in the late 1910s after emigrating from Japan. Prevented from purchasing land as an immigrant by the Alien Land Law of 1913, he secured a farm in central California by making his American-born children stockholders. He was an innovator in the industry, creating modern rice dryers and milling equipment.

In 1941, with the outbreak of the war with Japan, the American government sent the Koda family to internment camps in Colorado and forced them to hand over their business operations to non-Asians. When they were released in 1945, they found that much of their equipment had been sold. Keisaburo's sons rebuilt the business, and today, Keisaburo's grandchildren Ross and Robin operate Koda Farms.

Added-Value Rice

BAMBOO RICE

In China, you'll often see white rice infused with a chlorophyll-rich bamboo juice. At Lotus Foods, we import a sushi-style rice from family farms in northeast China infused with bamboo extract to give it a pale jade color, notes of vanilla, as well as beneficial phytonutrients. We call our green rice Jade Pearl Rice™.

BROKEN RICE

Rice grains broken during harvest or the milling process are separated out and sold separately. They are less expensive and often used in porridges, like congee. In the South, these broken grains are known as rice middlins or rice grits.

ENRICHED WHITE RICE

To replace some of the nutrients lost during the milling process, white rice grown in the United States must be enriched with B vitamins and iron and sometimes have other nutrients added, like zinc and folate. Much of the white rice sold in supermarkets and Asian markets is enriched white rice grown in California.

HAIGA MAI RICE

This semi-polished Japanese rice has the quick-cooking qualities of white rice but some of the nutrition and flavor of brown. It undergoes a special milling process to remove some of the bran layer but not the nutritious germ, giving you the best of both worlds.

PARBOILED RICE

Parboiled rice (also known as converted rice) is partially boiled while still in the husk to improve its shelf stability and nutritional value. The original technique dates back centuries in India. In North America, the rice industry adopted the technique and sometimes takes it further by precooking it more fully before drying so the rice cooks faster in your kitchen. Some rice lovers swear by using parboiled rice in one-pot dishes because it cooks without becoming mushy. Others think the rice—which is firm and very separate—is of inferior quality.

SPROUTED RICE

Whole-grain rice that is soaked until it starts germinating and then dried again before packaging can have more fiber than white rice and more bioavailable micronutrients. The process results in softer, less chewy brown rice that people often find easier to digest. Sprouted rice is sometimes marketed as GABA rice because the soaking process can increase gamma-aminobutyric acid (GABA), an amino acid shown to have a calming effect on the nerves. Sprouted rice rose in popularity at first with the macrobiotic diet, but it's now appealing to more people because it can cook faster than other whole-grain rice.

HOW TO COOK RICE

One of the complaints we hear most often from our customers is how stressed they feel cooking rice properly. We get it: There are many different methods and even more types of rice, and each can benefit from slightly different treatment. Rice cookery is part science and part tradition, with some spirituality woven in as well.

Here's the thing: If you start with a good-quality rice and follow the absorption method on the stove top and the water-to-rice ratios in the chart we provide on page 48, you will get a good pot of rice with evenly tender but not exceptionally firm grains. We have this recommendation on our packaging, and we stand by it. (One caveat is sticky rice, as glutinous rice must be steamed to get the right texture.)

We also realize some cooks like more dry, al dente rice while others prefer it even softer or more soupy. We encourage you to experiment with slightly different amounts of water and slightly different cooking times to find what you like best.

For those who would like to go deeper into rice-cooking theory, we're happy to share what we've learned over the years. Like any skill, rice cookery is about practice. Over time, you'll hone your intuition until you can cook transcendent rice every time.

THE INEXTRICABLE LINK BETWEEN WATER AND RICE

Rice, like life itself, is impossible without water. We need fresh water to grow rice and to cook it. But rice does not need as much water in the fields as we think. The image of the shimmering flooded rice paddy has become part of the romance of the landscape in rice-growing countries. Many varieties of rice naturally tolerate copious amounts of water, making it a good crop to grow where flooding occurs periodically. Many rice growers flood their fields because it's a straightforward way to keep weeds at bay. Rice, however, is not an aquatic plant.

Right now, each year, irrigating rice consumes half the world's renewable supply of fresh water used in global agriculture, which translates to one-quarter to one-third of the world's annual renewable supply of fresh water. As the world's demand for rice increases, that figure will grow, but it is neither sustainable nor necessary. As many rice-growing regions around the world see drastic drops in their water supply (in some cases directly due to rice production), farmers realize they cannot continue growing rice the same way. Increasingly, the agricultural research and development community is exploring innovative approaches to rice production that require less water, such as alternate wetting and drying patterns of irrigation, drip irrigation, direct seeding rather than transplanting, and the System of Rice Intensification (SRI), which was expressly developed for smallholder farmers and uses on average 25 to 50 percent less water. (To read more about SRI, see page 55.)

By sourcing rice from farmers using SRI methods, we estimate that Lotus Foods saves 500 million gallons of fresh water annually. To help people understand the benefit of the method easily, we trademarked the slogan More Crop Per Drop™. We hope as you cook rice, you'll think about the precious fresh water that has gone into growing it and choose to purchase rice from growers who value water conservation as well as other sustainable methods of agriculture.

To Rinse or Not to Rinse Your Rice

In many parts of the world, washing rice is often thought of as a meditative ritual as much as a practical one. It is done to remove loose and unwelcome pieces of hull and debris as well as any starch on the exterior of the rice. While most rice sold in the United States is generally clean of debris and is no longer coated with added starches like talc, people continue the process partially because of habit. Plus, washing rice can remove some impurities like arsenic (a concern for some rice, see page 153) as well as the loose starch on the grains produced when the rice gets agitated during transport. Some cooks who wash rice think it prepares the grains to start soaking up water during the cooking process and ultimately improves the texture and flavor of the finished rice. In the United States, some rice purveyors recommend against washing white rice because it removes the added enrichment.

Our view: If you're cooking white rice and hoping for separate grains or grains that cling together slightly but are not clumpy, sticky, or gluey, washing does help. To do so, put your rice in a bowl and cover with cold water. Use your fingers to agitate the rice, then drain the cloudy water. (You can water your plants with it if you like.) Repeat a few more times until the water is significantly less cloudy; it will not be totally clear. Drain the rice and allow it to sit in a strainer for a few minutes to remove any excess water.

Whole-grain rice is more forgiving to cook, even when you don't rinse it extensively. But because brown rice can harbor more metals from the soil than white rice does, it can be wise to wash it. One rice we never wash is our Jade Pearl Rice™ because it removes the bamboo extract and subtle green coloring.

To Soak or Not to Soak Your Rice

Cooks soak rice for many different reasons. Some feel that the grains cook more evenly because they're slightly hydrated when they hit the pot. The farmers who grow the basmati rice we sell always soak their rice for a little while before cooking, and we will say that the method produces spectacular results.

Some cooks soak whole-grain rice for several hours to transform the grains from dormant into activated seeds. By kickstarting germination, this process is thought to increase the nutritional value of the rice by making some of the micronutrients more bioavailable. There's also research that shows that soaking rice reduces the glycemic index slightly.

When you cook rice in a rice cooker, many machines have a soaking period built into the cycle.

After soaking, be sure to drain the rice well, letting it sit in a strainer for several minutes to remove excess water. Then decrease the amount of water you use in the cooking process slightly (by ¼ cup [60 ml]) and the time you spend cooking it.

To Season or Not to Season

Seasoning rice before you cook it is a personal preference. It's best to leave it without much seasoning when you want it to serve as a mild-tasting counterpoint to deliciously pungent flavors of the other food. If you're making a one-pot dish in which rice is one of the many ingredients, you'll likely want to season it well. When cooking a pot of rice, we like to add a few pinches of salt to the cooking water because it awakens the flavors of the rice.

How to Store Rice

To store your rice, keep it in an airtight container in a dark cabinet or the freezer. (Freezing rice also helps preserve the nutritious germ in whole-grain rice longer.)

You can refrigerate cooked rice in an airtight container for up to 2 days and freeze it for up to 3 months.

Basic Cooking Methods

Some of the recipes in this book include instructions for cooking the rice within the recipe because it's cooked with fat in a flavorful liquid. Other recipes call for cooked rice. At home, we cook most of our rice on the stove top using the absorption method (see below). If we're cooking a larger batch of rice, we use our rice cooker, and we know some cooks who swear by cooking rice in their Instant Pots. As with pasta, the best texture for rice is the one you like best. We know some cooks who prefer their rice so al dente, it's almost crunchy—many people would consider this rice undercooked. Don't be afraid to experiment to find what you like best.

WATER-TO-RICE RATIOS

Even if you always buy the same type of rice, the water-to-rice ratio can vary slightly depending on a myriad of factors: the quality of the harvest, the humidity of the storage area, and the age of the rice. In his book *My Korea*, chef Hooni Kim describes how he and his staff always cook a test batch from each new 50 lb [22.5 kg] bag of rice to determine the perfect water ratio—a step he says ensures consistent rice. Unlike chefs, most home cooks purchase smaller bags of rice, so a test batch for each bag is not practical.

Our advice: Get to know a few brands and styles of rice intimately and play around. Start with our recommended ratios but know that you can always decrease or add water and time depending on whether you like firmer or more tender grains of rice. Remember: It's a personal preference.

STOVE TOP ABSORPTION

When using a stove top, it's important to use a heavy pot with a tight-fitting lid so that your rice cooks evenly. The heavy pot retains the heat while the lid does not allow much steam to escape. Choose a pot that will hold at least three times the volume of dried rice with a bit of space above it, as the rice will expand as it cooks.

In the pot, cover the rice with water (see Cooking Chart page 48) and add some salt, if desired. Over medium-high heat, bring the water to a near boil, turn the heat to low so the water is barely simmering, and cover with a lid. Cook for the designated amount of time (see Cooking Chart; timing may vary depending on the brand of rice), then turn off the heat. If there's so much steam coming out of the pot while cooking that the lid is shaking, lower the heat.

When cooking rice, it's important to keep the lid on to prevent evaporation, but it's okay to uncover the pot quickly once or twice to check its progress. (You'll likely want to do this when you're cooking a new whole-grain rice to get an idea of how long you should let it simmer, as it can vary from brand to brand.) When the rice is tender, remove the pot from the heat and keep it covered for 5 minutes for white rice and up to 10 minutes for whole-grain rice. This last step might be the most important, as it gives rice a chance to steam, fully hydrate, and become fluffy. Don't let it stand covered too long, however, or it can become mushy. Use a fork, wooden spoon, or rice paddle to fluff before serving.

BOILING

Yes, you can boil rice like pasta. This method works well for rice salads, or you can parboil rice before adding it to a dish to finish cooking through. We also recommend this method if arsenic is a concern; when the excess water is drained off, it can reduce the amount of arsenic left in the rice. (See page 153 for more about rice and arsenic.)

To use this method, bring a large pot of salted water to a boil, add the rice, and cook until just tender, 10 to 15 minutes for white rice and 20 to 35 minutes for whole-grain rice. (When you bite a grain, it should be translucent throughout with no opaqueness in the center.) Drain in a colander and rinse.

STEAMING (FOR STICKY RICE)

Soak sticky rice for 4 to 12 hours before cooking, then drain. Line a large steamer basket or fine-mesh sieve with cheesecloth or a damp kitchen towel so it hangs over the edges. Add the rice to the cloth. Using a pot large enough to hold the steamer basket or sieve, add 1 in [2.5 cm] of water and set the basket over the water. Bring the water to a boil over high heat, then lower the heat to medium. Cover and steam the rice for 15 minutes. Remove the cheesecloth with the rice from the steamer basket and use the overhang of the cheesecloth to carefully flip the solid disk of sticky rice onto a plate. Return the cheesecloth to the basket and the rice to the cheesecloth so the cooked side is now up, then return the basket to the pot. Steam the rice until cooked through but not mushy, 10 to 15 minutes longer. Use a fork, wooden spoon, or rice paddle to fluff before serving.

RICE COOKER

In a rice cooker, cover the rice with water and add a pinch of salt, if desired. We use the same water ratio in the rice cooker as we do on the stove top (see page 48), but we know some people recommend using less water. See your manufacturer's instructions and feel free to experiment.

To cook the rice, turn on the cooker and select the correct cooking method according to the manufacturer's instructions. If you have already soaked your rice, choose a quick-cooking setting,

STOVE TOP COOKING CHART

TYPE OF RICE	AMOUNT OF DRY RICE	AMOUNT OF WATER	COOKING TIME	YIELD
Short-grain white rice (including sushi rice and Jade Pearl Rice™)	1 cup [200 g]	1⅓ cups [320 ml] for unsoaked rice and 1 cup plus 2 Tbsp [270 ml] for soaked rice	10 to 15 minutes plus 5 minutes resting	2 cups [360 g]
	1½ cups [300 g]	2 cups [480 ml] for unsoaked rice and 1¾ cups [415 ml] for soaked rice	10 to 15 minutes plus 5 minutes resting	3 cups [540 g]
	2 cups [400 g]	2⅔ cups [640 ml] for unsoaked rice and 2½ cups [600 ml] for soaked rice	10 to 15 minutes plus 5 minutes resting	4 cups [720 g]
Medium- and long-grain white rice (including jasmine and basmati)	1 cup [200 g]	1½ cups [360 ml] for unsoaked rice and 1¼ cups [300 ml] for soaked rice	20 minutes plus 5 minutes resting	About 3 cups [360 g]
	1½ cups [300 g]	2¼ cups [540 ml] for unsoaked rice and 2 cups [480 ml] for soaked rice	20 minutes plus 5 minutes resting	About 4½ cups [540 g]
	2 cups [400 g]	3 cups [720 ml] for unsoaked rice and 2¾ cups [660 ml] for soaked rice	20 minutes plus 5 minutes resting	About 6 cups [720 g]

TYPE OF RICE	AMOUNT OF DRY RICE	AMOUNT OF WATER	COOKING TIME	YIELD
Short-grain and long-grain brown rice	1 cup [200 g]	1¾ cups [420 ml] for unsoaked rice and 1½ cups [360 ml] for soaked rice	30 to 45 minutes plus 5 to 10 minutes resting	2 to 3 cups [360 g]
	1½ cups [300 g]	2⅔ cup [640 ml] for unsoaked rice and 2¼ cup [540 ml] for soaked rice	30 to 45 minutes plus 5 to 10 minutes resting	3 to 4½ cups [540 g]
	2 cups [400 g]	3½ cups [840 ml] for unsoaked rice and 3¼ cups [780 ml] for soaked rice	30 to 45 minutes plus 5 to 10 minutes resting	4 to 6 cups [720 g]
Red rice and black rice	1 cup [200 g]	1¾ cups [420 ml] for unsoaked rice and 1½ cups [360 ml] for soaked rice	30 minutes, plus 5 to 10 minutes resting	About 3 cups [360 g]
	1½ cups [300 g]	2⅔ cup [640 ml] for unsoaked rice and 2¼ cups [540 ml] for soaked rice	30 minutes, plus 5 to 10 minutes resting	About 4½ cups [540 g]
	2 cups [400 g]	3½ cups [840 ml] for unsoaked rice and 3¼ cups [780 ml] for soaked rice	30 minutes, plus 5 to 10 minutes resting	About 6 cups [720 g]

PRESSURE COOKER CHART

TYPE OF RICE	AMOUNT OF DRY RICE	AMOUNT OF WATER	COOKING TIME	YIELD
Short-grain white rice (including sushi rice and Jade Pearl Rice™)	1 cup [200 g]	1 cup [240 ml]	6 minutes on high pressure, let pressure release naturally	2 cups [360 g]
Medium- and long-grain white rice (including jasmine and basmati)	1 cup [200 g]	1 cup plus 2 Tbsp [270 ml]	6 minutes on high pressure, let pressure release naturally	About 3 cups [360 g]
Whole-grain rice, such as brown, rice, red rice, and black rice	1 cup [200 g]	1¼ cups [300 ml]	15 minutes on high pressure, let pressure release naturally	About 3 cups [360 g]

as many rice cookers are programmed to soak rice first. Some rice cookers have brown rice settings, which you can use for any whole-grain rice, including black or red rice. The rice cooker will automatically turn off when the rice is done. Let it stand for 5 minutes, then open the lid and use a fork, wooden spoon, or rice paddle to fluff before serving.

ELECTRIC PRESSURE COOKER

Electric pressure cookers, such as Instant Pots, allow you to cook rice quickly without needing to hover over the pot. Because of the pressure in the pot, you can use less water.

NOTE If the rice sits in the warm pot for an extended period after cooking, it can dry out on top and become mushy on the bottom.

HOW TO CHOOSE A RICE COOKER

There are basic rice cookers with nothing more than an on/off switch, and deluxe models that practically promise to do your laundry for you in addition to all the different settings for cooking rice. Here are some parameters to consider as you choose your rice cooker.

CAPACITY
If you have a small household and typically cook 1 to 1½ cups [200 to 300 g] of dried rice at a time, look for compact cookers with a 6 cup [1.4 L] capacity. If you like to cook big batches, choose cookers with a 10 cup [2.4 L] or more capacity.

THE LID
Cookers with removable lids are easier to clean.

MATERIAL OF THE BOWL
Many rice cooker bowls have nonstick coatings, which can degrade over time. If you're nervous about nonstick coatings, seek out rice cookers made with stainless steel or clay bowls.

ADDITIONAL ACCESSORIES
Some rice cookers come with trays so you can use your cooker to steam other ingredients.

SETTINGS
Choose a rice cooker that has a "quick rice" setting if you prefer to soak rice on your own; otherwise, the cooker might be programmed to soak the rice before you cook it. More expensive cookers employ fuzzy logic technology, which makes micro adjustments to help you achieve perfect rice. Many of these cookers also have a variety of settings for different varieties of rice. To be honest, we're minimalists at heart and love using basic rice cookers with simple on/off switches. Regardless, we find once you get to know your machine, you can cook perfect rice every time.

FOR THE LOVE OF CRISPY RICE

"The crispy rice that can form on the bottom of the pot always conjures up memories of when, as an extended family of nine, we would roll the crispy bits and the softer bits into an egg-like shape and enjoy them that way," says Ken. Many different cultures value the crispy, chewy, nutty, slightly scorched rice that forms on the bottom of the pot—whether it's created on purpose or by accident. In Korea, it's known as nurungji; in Japan, okoge; and in Ghana, it's kanzo. In Latin America, it often goes by pegao (a shortened version of pegado, Spanish for "stuck") and a few other different names. Persian cooks are often judged by the quality of their tahdig—the thin, golden crust of crispy rice—and how well it releases from the pot.

There are a few different ways to create some version of this crispy layer, including fortunate happenstance. One is to simply cook rice on the stove top while covered for 10 minutes longer than indicated. Pull out the unscorched rice, then add a little water to the pot to loosen the chewy browned rice on the bottom.

You can also start with cooked rice and toast it in a dry pan or with a little oil, pressing it into an even layer if you like. This will make the rice crispier. "If you like, you can make jook or congee from the crispy bits at the bottom by adding plenty of liquid to the rice and cooking until it becomes a porridge. The bits add a smoky flavor," Ken says.

For tahdig, cooks usually add fat to the rice after it's plumped in water and then cook it over very low heat while covered until the beautiful crusty layer forms. After the tahdig forms, cooks invert the pan onto a plate to unmold the rice cake in the hopes they created a golden, unbroken layer.

TROUBLESHOOTING

MY RICE IS TOO STICKY

This might sound obvious, but double check whether you purchased something called sticky, glutinous, or sweet rice. This rice is stickier and benefits from steaming. If you have a non-sticky rice, try rinsing it well next time (see page 41). You can also try using less water when cooking.

MY RICE IS UNDERCOOKED

After rice is done simmering, be sure to let it steam in the pot off the heat for 5 to 10 minutes. This is a crucial step and often helps the rice cook through and absorb the last bit of liquid. If that doesn't help, check the water level. If the pot is dry, add 2 Tbsp of water and return it to the heat for another 5 to 10 minutes, then check again. If that helps, increase your water amount next time with that variety of rice.

MY RICE IS MUSHY

Try cooking it for less time with slightly less water next time. Also, after your rice steams off the heat—5 minutes for white rice and up to 10 minutes for whole-grain rice—uncover the pot.

MY RICE IS WET

If there is still liquid left in your pot after you've removed it from the heat to let it steam, drain it off and decrease the amount of water next time. You can also return the rice to the heat, uncovered, and cook briefly for a minute or two to allow the last bit of water to evaporate.

MY RICE IS SCORCHED

If the rice on the bottom of the pot burns, taste the rice from the top of the pot. If it tastes okay, remove the rice from the top of the pot and serve that. Some people prize slightly scorched rice for its chewy texture and nutty flavor, but rice that's burned black tastes acrid (see For the Love of Crispy Rice, facing page). Pull off a piece of the scorched rice and taste it. If you like the texture and flavor, serve it. If not, discard. Either way, add a little water to the pot and return it to the heat to help loosen the scorched rice from the bottom. And to avoid scorched rice in the future, use lower heat and consider switching to a pot with a heavier bottom for cooking rice.

1

EGGS
AND RICE

A NEW DAY, A NEW WAY
OF GROWING RICE

At first, it sounded too good to be true.

In 2005, we received a call from Olivia Vent at Cornell University, who told us about a method for growing rice that required less seed, less water, and no agrochemical inputs, such as fertilizers, pesticides, and herbicides. Called the System of Rice Intensification (SRI), this regenerative agriculture methodology results in healthier rice plants with deeper root systems and, better yet, more rice for the farmers.

We knew we had to see it for ourselves. In 2006, we traveled to Madagascar, where the methodology was developed, and in 2007, we visited Cambodia. In these countries, we met farmers who showed us the novel practices in their fields and attested to the dramatic yield increases even using their traditional seeds, without need for new "improved" seeds or agrochemical inputs. With more rice to eat and surplus to sell, they were able to improve their overall lives. As we dug deeper, we also learned that growing rice conventionally uses up to one-third of the planet's renewable supply of fresh water each year (yes, one-third!) and adds a significant amount of methane—one of the major climate-warming gases—to the atmosphere.

After we saw SRI in action, we committed that every new rice we imported would be grown in this way, if possible. In 2009, we imported one container (18 metric tons) each of rice grown by farmers using SRI methods from Cambodia, Madagascar, and Indonesia. By importing rice from an estimated 2,500 SRI farmers between 2009 and 2019, our company and those who buy its products have saved over 4 billion gallons of fresh water (averaging about 500 million gallons annually).

The origins of SRI are surprising. A French Jesuit priest and trained agronomist, Fr. Henri de Laulanié, wanted to help rice growers in Madagascar, who depend on their crop for daily subsistence, improve their yields without needing to purchase expensive commercial products. Through years of experimentation in the 1970s and 1980s, he and local farmers learned that they could often increase their yields by double or more by changing how they grew rice. First, they transplanted rice seedlings at a younger age, in rows, and with more space between plants. This minimized transplant shock, reduced competition among plants, and facilitated weeding. Second, they controlled the water levels so the soil was moist but not flooded. And third, they focused on the health of the soil using organic inputs like compost. In the 1990s, he set up a nonprofit organization, Association Tefy Saina. It partnered in 1993 with the Cornell International Institute for Food, Agriculture and Development, which was seeking ways to help farmers in central Madagascar move away from slash-and-burn agriculture because of the way it diminishes rainforest ecosystems and biodiversity.

Keeping the fields irrigated but not flooded (see page 65) is better for the soil. Plus it reduces methane emissions, and means that more fresh water is available for other crops and natural areas, and to recharge wells, streams, and rivers. It also means the people working in the fields, mainly women, are less exposed to the diseases that can come from working in flooded water. Draining water from fields can also reduce mosquito populations.

What was intended as a strategy to improve food security for sub-sistence farmers became an opportunity to increase families' incomes, reduce freshwater usage, *and* combat climate change. Because of the way SRI can benefit farmers, communities, and ecosystems, local and international organizations such as Oxfam, SRI-Rice at Cornell University, World Wildlife Fund, CARE, the World Bank, and many others have helped spread the methodology to more than sixty countries, and its popularity only continues to grow.

BENEFITS OF THE SYSTEM OF RICE INTENSIFICATION (SRI)

CONVENTIONAL RICE GROWING	SRI GROWING PRACTICES
Seedling nurseries in flooded fields	Small seed beds with 80 to 90% fewer seeds
Seedlings transplanted at 21 to 45 days in clumps of 3 or more	Seedlings transplanted at 8 to 15 days, just 1 seedling per hill, with hills widely spaced
Transplanting into flooded or puddled fields	Transplanting into muddy but unflooded soil
Fields are kept flooded	Fields are alternately irrigated and drained
Hand weeding to control weeds	Upright push weeder aerates soil and removes weeds
Synthetic fertilizer, herbicides, and pesticides	Organic fertilizers, including compost, to build soil health

RICE, PEOPLE, PLANET	WHY WE'RE PASSIONATE ABOUT SRI
Rice is a daily food for half the world's people.	· Higher yields (50 to 100+%) with any variety; promotes food security and rice biodiversity
About half of all irrigation water is used for rice.	· Uses 25 to 50% less water
Flooded fields produce methane emmisions.	· 40+% reduction in methane emissions
Reliance on agrochemicals can be toxic.	· Improves soil health · Resistance to drought, pests, diseases, storms
Most rice is still produced on approximately 200 million family farms.	· Accessible to resource-limited families · More rice to eat and sell; more income
Women do most of the work to grow rice. (Farm productivity is linked to worker health.)	· Reduction in work and health hazards benefit women

ABOVE: A farmer in Odisha, India, practicing SRI methods, uses a simple rake to create a grid for the placement of the young, single seedlings at wide spacing and in rows.

TOP LEFT: Under SRI management, seedlings are uprooted at 8-15 days and planted one seedling per hill, rather than older seedlings in clumps. This reduces transplant shock and competition among plants.

TOP RIGHT: Indonesian farmer Miyatty Jannah holds a rice plant grown under SRI management (left) and a rice plant of the same age grown under conventional management (right).

BOTTOM RIGHT: SRI fields in West Java, Indonesia. Wider spacing of single seedlings means that farmers need 80 to 90 percent fewer seedlings—a huge cost savings that also leaves more rice for the family to eat.

BLACK RICE WITH BRUSSELS SPROUTS AND FRIED EGGS

SERVES 4

Almost any rice dish can be made more delicious with a fried egg, but for this one, it's especially true. The combination of lightly browned onions, sautéed Brussels sprouts, and creamy egg yolks is just magic. You can use day-old rice here, but you don't have to.

¼ cup plus 1 Tbsp [75 ml] extra-virgin olive oil

1 large yellow onion, halved and thinly sliced

Salt

1 lb [455 g] Brussels sprouts, halved lengthwise and thinly sliced crosswise

1 cup [200 g] Forbidden Rice® or other non-sticky black rice, cooked (see page 49)

1 lemon, zested

4 large eggs

In a large skillet over medium heat, warm ¼ cup [60 ml] of the olive oil. Add the onion, season generously with salt, and cook, stirring, until softened and lightly browned, about 10 minutes. Add the Brussels sprouts, season with salt, and cook, stirring, until just barely softened, about 4 minutes. Stir in the rice and cook until warmed through, about 1 minute. Add the lemon zest and the juice from half the lemon. Turn off the heat. Taste and add more lemon juice and season with more salt, if desired.

In another large nonstick skillet over medium heat, heat the remaining 1 Tbsp of olive oil. Crack the eggs in the skillet and cook, turning once, until the whites are set but the yolks are still runny, about 1 ½ minutes per side. (If you prefer sunny-side up eggs, see page 77.)

Transfer the black rice and Brussels sprouts to bowls, top with the fried eggs, and serve.

BLACK RICE PORRIDGE WITH
SEVEN-MINUTE EGGS AND CHILI CRISP

**SERVES
4**

Savory porridges are eaten throughout much of the world. Congee, which is usually made with white rice cooked with enough liquid so that it breaks down to form a silky, nearly smooth texture, is probably the most well known. There are endless variations on these porridges—sometimes they include meat, seafood, or vegetables. Other times, as in this recipe, they're left plain and then served with a few deeply flavorful toppings. Because this version is so plain, use the best chicken stock you can. (The stock left over from the Hainanese Chicken and Rice on page 198 works especially well.)

Black rice brings an incredible flavor and intriguing color to this porridge. Because the bran layer of the rice is left intact, the texture is a little bit chewier than you'll usually find with congee, but we find it to be incredibly satisfying.

Chili crisp is a spicy, crunchy sauce made by frying red chiles, garlic, shallots, Sichuan peppercorns, and other ingredients in oil so they become flavorful and crispy. Because of the Sichuan peppercorns, it has an enjoyable tongue-numbing quality that makes it hard to stop eating. While you can make your own, we like to use jarred versions we find at many Asian and specialty markets. We're particularly enamored with the chili crisp by Fly by Jing (flybyjing.com).

1 cup [200 g] Forbidden Rice® or other non-sticky black rice

8 cups [2 L] chicken stock (or a combination of chicken stock and water)

Salt

4 large eggs

Sliced green onions and Sichuan chili crisp, for serving

In a heavy saucepan over high heat, cover the rice with the chicken stock and bring to a boil. Stir the rice to make sure it's not sticking to the bottom, lower the heat to medium-low, and cover the pot. Cook, stirring every 20 to 30 minutes, until the grains of rice have burst and turned inside out, about 1 hour.

CONT'D

Uncover the pot and increase the heat to medium. Simmer the rice, stirring occasionally and adjusting the heat as necessary to stay under a boil, until the rice has a very loose porridge-like texture, 35 to 40 minutes. Season the porridge with salt.

Meanwhile, bring a medium saucepan of water to a boil over high heat. Lower the heat to medium to maintain a simmer and carefully add the eggs, making sure they are covered with the water. Simmer the eggs for 7 minutes, then drain. Return the eggs to the saucepan and cover with cold water to stop the cooking. When you're ready to peel, feel the eggs. If they are not warm to the touch, cover them with warm water and let stand for 5 minutes to warm them up. Carefully peel the eggs, cut them in half, and sprinkle with salt.

Spoon the porridge into bowls, arrange the egg halves on top, and garnish with green onions. Drizzle as much chili crisp over the bowls as you like and serve more at the table.

NOTE

If you prefer, you can make this porridge in an electric pressure cooker, such as an Instant Pot. In the pot, combine 1 cup [200 g] Forbidden Rice® or other nonsticky black rice with 5 cups stock or water and cook on high pressure for 1 hour. Let the pressure release naturally and stir. Add more liquid if you prefer a looser porridge.

RICE IS LIFE

SPICED LENTIL AND RICE "SHAKSHUKA"

SERVES 4

Throughout North Africa and parts of the Middle East, you'll find variations of a dish known as shakshuka—eggs gently cooked in a tomato sauce, often made with peppers. Here, red lentils and basmati rice join the tomato sauce, breaking down and cooking together, becoming almost creamy. For a delicious counterpoint, you can serve the shakshuka with thick Greek-style yogurt or sprinkles of feta cheese. This is a comforting one-pot meal you can eat any time of day.

¼ cup [60 ml] extra-virgin olive oil

1 large yellow onion, chopped

2 garlic cloves, smashed and chopped

Salt

1 tsp ground coriander

1 tsp yellow mustard seeds

½ tsp ground cumin

1 cup [240 ml] tomato passata (uncooked tomato purée)

1 cup [200 g] red lentils

½ cup [100 g] white basmati rice

1 qt [960 ml] chicken or vegetable broth

Finely grated orange zest

2 cups [30 g] baby kale or 4 cups [80 g] baby spinach, rinsed

Freshly ground pepper

4 large eggs

4 oz [115 g] crumbled feta, for serving

Chopped cilantro, for serving

In a deep, wide skillet over medium heat, warm the oil. Add the onion and garlic, season generously with salt, and cook, stirring occasionally, until softened, about 8 minutes. Add the coriander, mustard seed, and cumin and cook, stirring, until fragrant, about 1 minute. Add the tomato passata and bring to a simmer. Add the lentils, rice, and broth and stir. Bring to a boil over high heat, then lower the heat to medium-low, cover, and simmer for 15 minutes. Stir in the orange zest and scrape the bottom of the skillet to make sure nothing is scorching, then add the kale on top. Cover and simmer for 5 minutes. Stir in the kale, then taste the rice and lentils and season with salt and pepper. Make four wells in the top of the rice mixture. Crack an egg into each well and cover the skillet. Cook until the egg whites are set and the yolks are still runny, 8 to 12 minutes, depending on the size of the eggs. Season the eggs with salt.

Scoop the shakshuka into bowls, sprinkle with feta and cilantro, and serve.

KEN'S FRIED RICE

**SERVES
2 TO 4**

Growing up, Ken's father and his four brothers owned a Chinese restaurant in Providence, Rhode Island, and throughout most of his life, he enjoyed his family's delicious food. When Ken was about to move to Houston for a job, he realized he didn't know how to cook any of the dishes his father made, so he asked his dad to teach him how to cook fried rice.

His father showed him how to prepare each ingredient with respect for its individuality so it would cook properly and contribute to a harmonious whole. "I realized later that he was teaching me about life, about the importance of blending in with people, of accommodating different kinds of conversations that are inclusive," says Ken.

Ken now uses his father's method but not the same ingredients. Instead, he makes fried rice with what he has on hand, including vegetables Caryl grows in the garden. In spring, he reaches for asparagus, chives, and leafy greens. He adds the asparagus toward the beginning of cooking so it's cooked through. If you like more al dente asparagus, add it just before adding the eggs.

To create your own version, use this recipe as well as the tips on page 71.

2 large eggs

Salt

2 Tbsp peanut or rice bran oil

1 small yellow onion, chopped

2 garlic cloves, finely grated

1 tsp finely grated fresh ginger (from 1 in [2.5 cm] peeled ginger)

1 lb [455 g] medium-thick asparagus, ends trimmed and spears cut crosswise into ½ in [13 mm] lengths

4 cups [about 480 g] cooked, cooled rice (see page 48; use day-old rice if it's white)

One 5 oz [140 g] bag baby spinach

2 Tbsp soy sauce or tamari, or 1 Tbsp soy sauce blended with 1 Tbsp oyster sauce

Chopped chives or green onion tops, for serving

CONT'D

Lightly beat the eggs with ¼ tsp of salt.

In a well-seasoned wok or large, deep skillet (not nonstick) over high heat, warm the oil until shimmering. Have a lid that fits over the top of the wok nearby.

Add the onion, season with salt, if desired, and stir-fry until the onion is bright white and opaque and just starting to soften, 1 to 2 minutes. Add the garlic and ginger and stir-fry until fragrant, about 20 seconds. Stir in the asparagus, then push the vegetables to the side of the wok to form a well in the center.

Add the rice and several pinches of salt, if desired, to the well and use a spatula to press down the rice to quickly heat it and break up any clumps, about 20 seconds. Push the vegetables up and over the rice, then spread out the rice and cover the wok. Cook, until you hear the rice start to crackle, 10 to 20 seconds. Uncover and use the spatula to flip the rice in large sections so the rice on the bottom is now toward the top; the rice should be a bit browned on the bottom in spots. Press the rice into an even layer to work out any clumps, cover the wok again, and cook until it begins to crackle, 10 to 20 seconds.

Push the fried rice to the side of the pan to form a well in the center. Add the eggs to the well and cook, without stirring, until they start to set on the bottom, about 30 seconds; stir to allow the unset egg to cook, creating medium to large curds of scrambled eggs.

Use the spatula to push the vegetables and rice on top of the eggs, then stir-fry to incorporate the egg curds; continue to press the rice to remove any clumps as you see them, about 10 seconds.

Add the spinach, in batches if necessary, and stir-fry until the leaves are barely wilted, about 10 seconds. Pour in the soy sauce around the edges of the wok or skillet so it hits the surface of the pan. Stir the sauce into the rice until incorporated. Remove the fried rice from the heat. Taste and season with a little salt, if desired. The rice should taste seasoned but not overly salty so the delicate flavors of the rice, eggs, and vegetables can come through.

Sprinkle with chives and serve.

TIPS FOR FRIED RICE

USE DAY-OLD RICE IF IT'S WHITE

Fried rice should be fluffy, dry, and a little bit crispy. The best way to achieve that texture with white rice is to use day-old rice that's been refrigerated. If you'd like to cool down rice quickly to use for fried rice, spread it out on a baking sheet and let stand at room temperature for up to 1 hour. Whole-grain rice, including brown, red, and black, works well in fried rice, even when it's freshly cooked, as long as it's not wet.

PREP ALL YOUR INGREDIENTS AHEAD

Cooking fried rice moves lightning fast. Have ingredients prepped and sauces mixed before you heat the oil.

ADD INGREDIENTS IN THE RIGHT ORDER

Ken starts with the aromatic vegetables, like onions, garlic, and ginger. He then follows up with firmer vegetables, such as carrots or celery. He finishes with quick-cooking vegetables, like frozen peas or tender leafy greens.

COOK EGGS SO THEY FORM LARGE CURDS

You do not want the eggs to coat every ingredient but rather form their own curds that get mixed into the rice. Some people achieve this by cooking the eggs first, then removing them from the pan and adding them back in. Ken prefers to scramble the eggs as he cooks the fried rice, but he creates a well in the center of the pan so they can cook without coating the other ingredients.

USE A WOK OR LARGE CAST-IRON SKILLET

A wok or cast-iron skillet will help you achieve the heat level needed for fried rice.

USE HIGH HEAT

Ken is always seeking *wok hey*, a Cantonese term that literally means "breath of a wok" and figuratively refers to an ineffable flavor that comes from high-heat wok cooking. While it's challenging to achieve wok hey on a home stove, you can get close by using high heat.

OMURICE

SERVES 2 TO 4

This might be the dish that ends the debate about whether eggs and ketchup go together. In this dish, they do. A Japanese favorite, *omurice* literally translates to "omelet and rice" and that's what it is: fried rice (often sauced with ketchup) draped with a gently cooked omelet of sorts.

This recipe makes two plates of omurice, which you can put in the center of the table to serve four people family style.

5 green onions	3 slices deli ham, cut into bite-size pieces
5 Tbsp [75 g] ketchup	
4 tsp soy sauce, plus more as needed	3 cups [about 360 g] cooked, cooled rice, any type
3 Tbsp canola oil or butter	4 large eggs
½ small head green cabbage, shredded	Salt

Thinly slice the green onions, keeping the dark green parts separate.

In a small bowl, combine 3 Tbsp of the ketchup with 2 tsp of the soy sauce.

In a wok or deep skillet over medium-high heat, warm 2 Tbsp of the oil. Add the white and light green parts of the green onions and cook, stirring, until softened, about 2 minutes. Add the cabbage and cook, stirring, until softened and no longer raw tasting, about 5 minutes. Stir in the deli ham followed by the rice and stir until everything is incorporated and warmed through. Add the ketchup mixture and stir until the rice is pink. Taste and add more soy sauce, if desired. Add the dark green parts of the green onions and toss. Turn off the heat and keep warm.

In a bowl, whisk together 2 of the eggs with ⅛ tsp of salt.

72

In a small nonstick skillet over medium heat, warm ½ Tbsp of the oil. Add the whisked eggs and cook, moving the skillet around and stirring, until the eggs are creamy but still loose, about 1 minute. Tilt the skillet to spread the eggs into an even layer and let cook, mostly undisturbed, just tilting the skillet occasionally to allow the uncooked eggs to flow toward the edges to set. When the bottom of the eggs is set (but not browned) and the top is custardy, about 1 minute longer, remove from the heat.

TO SERVE, scoop half of the fried rice into a cereal bowl and press in tightly. Invert the rice onto a plate. Repeat with the remaining rice on a separate plate, keeping it covered with the bowl to keep warm.

Invert the eggs over one mound of rice so they're custardy-side down, covering the rice completely. Use a clean towel to fix the placement of the omelet and tuck the edges under the rice, if desired.

Whisk together the remaining 2 eggs with ⅛ tsp of salt and repeat cooking the eggs with the remaining ½ Tbsp of oil. Remove the bowl from the second mound of rice and drape the eggs over the rice.

In a small bowl, stir together the remaining 2 Tbsp of ketchup and 2 tsp of soy sauce. Dollop or spread over the eggs and serve family style.

BREAKFAST SAUSAGE FRIED RICE

SERVES 2 TO 4

Fried rice is wonderful any time of day, but here is one you might want to make for breakfast. For the sausage, you can use any type you prefer, including vegetarian. If you like a little sweetness in the morning, you can mix 1 or 2 tsp of maple syrup into the soy sauce before adding it to the fried rice.

5 green onions

2 large eggs

Salt

8 oz [230 g] tender mustard greens, spinach, or baby kale

3 Tbsp canola oil

7 to 8 oz [200 to 230g] breakfast sausage links, sliced crosswise into coins

2 garlic cloves, finely grated

1 tsp finely grated fresh ginger (from 1 in [2.5 cm] peeled ginger)

4 cups [about 480 g] cooked rice (see page 48; use day-old rice if it's white)

3 Tbsp soy sauce, plus more as needed

Chili-garlic sauce or sambal ulek, for serving

Thinly slice the green onions, keeping the dark green parts separate. Lightly beat the eggs with ¼ tsp salt.

In a wok or well-seasoned cast-iron skillet over medium heat, combine the mustard greens with 2 Tbsp of water, cover, and steam until wilted, about 1 minute. Transfer to a cutting board and let cool, then squeeze out any excess moisture and coarsely chop.

In the same wok over high heat, warm 1 Tbsp of the oil. Add the sausage in a single layer and cook, without moving, until browned on the bottom, about 3 minutes. Stir once or twice, then add the white and light green parts of the green onions and stir-fry until softened, about 1 minute. Add the garlic and ginger and stir-fry until no longer raw smelling, about 30 seconds.

Add 1 Tbsp of the oil and heat for 10 seconds, then add the rice and stir to incorporate with the ingredients. Spread the rice in an even layer and use a spatula to press down the rice to quickly heat it and break up any clumps, about 20 seconds. Flip the rice up and over itself a few times, then press it down again in spots to work out any remaining clumps and get a bit crispy. Season the rice with salt.

Push all the ingredients to the side of the wok to form a well in the center. Add the remaining 1 Tbsp of oil to the well and heat for about 10 seconds. Add the eggs to the well and cook, without stirring, until they start to set on the bottom. Stir to allow any unset egg to cook, creating medium to large curds of scrambled eggs.

Use the spatula to push the egg curds over the rice, then stir-fry, continuing to press out any clumps of rice as you see them, about 30 seconds. Add the chopped greens to the fried rice.

Pour in the soy sauce around the edges of the wok or skillet so it hits the surface of the pan, stir it in, and turn off the heat. Taste and add more soy sauce, if desired.

Transfer the fried rice to bowls, garnish with the dark green parts of the green onions, and serve with chili-garlic sauce.

CENTRAL JAVANESE NASI GORENG

SERVES 2 TO 4

We partner with a group of farmers in Central Java in Indonesia where the go-to dish is fried rice, known in Indonesia as nasi goreng. The distinctive sweet-salty-umami flavor of this version of nasi goreng comes from a concentrated sweet soy sauce, called kecap manis, as well as shrimp paste or fish sauce.

There are countless versions of this dish, with some including chicken, seafood, or seasonal vegetables. This recipe is quite simple but is topped with the quintessential fried egg. Cooked with chiles, the rice should be a little bit spicy. For a spicier dish, serve sambal ulek alongside. (The Hot Chili Sambal from Auria's Malaysian Kitchen, a Brooklyn, New York–based company founded by chef Auria Abraham, is especially good.)

5 Tbsp [75 ml] canola oil

1 large shallot, finely chopped

6 garlic cloves, finely chopped

1 to 2 long, thin chiles, thinly sliced

2 tsp Indonesian or Thai shrimp paste or fish sauce

4 cups [480 g] cooked rice (see page 48; use day-old rice if it's white)

2 Tbsp kecap manis (see Note)

1 Tbsp soy sauce

4 green onions, thinly sliced

4 large eggs

Flaky salt, for sprinkling

Sliced cucumber, lime wedges, and sambal ulek, for serving

In a wok or large skillet over high heat, warm 2 Tbsp of oil until shimmering. Add the shallot, garlic, and chiles and stir-fry until softened, 30 seconds to 1 minute. Add the shrimp paste and cook, stirring it into the oil and breaking it up with a spoon to help it incorporate, 30 seconds to 1 minute. Add the rice and stir-fry while using a spoon to break up any clumps and pressing the rice into the wok to heat it through. Stir in the kecap manis and soy sauce and cook, stirring, just until incorporated and slightly thickened, then turn off the heat and stir in the sliced green onions.

You can purchase kecap manis at many Asian markets and some well-stocked supermarkets. You can also make an approximation of it yourself. In a small saucepan over medium heat, combine ¼ cup [60 ml] of soy sauce with ¼ cup plus 2 Tbsp [80 g] of brown sugar and bring to a simmer. Carefully maintain the heat so the mixture simmers at the edges but does not boil over. Whisk until the sauce is thickened like syrup and looks wrinkled when you tilt the pan, 1 to 2 minutes. Let cool completely, then measure out 2 Tbsp and reserve the rest for another use.

Meanwhile, in a large, well-seasoned cast-iron or nonstick skillet over medium-high heat, warm 3 Tbsp of oil until shimmering. Crack the eggs in the skillet and cook, allowing the bottoms and edges to brown and the edges to turn lacy. Carefully tip the skillet and spoon some of the hot oil over the top of the eggs to help the rest of the egg whites set. When the egg whites are set but the yolks are still runny, transfer the eggs to a plate and sprinkle with flaky salt.

Transfer the fried rice to plates, top with the eggs, and serve with sliced cucumber, lime wedges, and sambal ulek.

HOW TO COOK A SUNNY-SIDE-UP EGG

Hate to flip your eggs? Or maybe you just love the look of that sunny yolk? Even within the category of sunny-side-up eggs, there are a few different sub-categories. Do you like crispy-edged eggs, or do you believe eggs should never brown? Do you find the bottoms get overcooked while the tops stay gooey? Here are a few tips.

FOR CRISPY-EDGED EGGS Add an additional 1 Tbsp of oil to the skillet and cook the eggs over medium-high heat, allowing the eggs to brown on the bottom. (Use a screen if you have one to prevent hot oil spatters.) Occasionally tilt the skillet and spoon the oil over the tops of the eggs to help the whites set and create crispy, lacy edges.

FOR WHITE SUNNY-SIDE-UP EGGS Cook the eggs over medium heat until the bottoms are set. Lower the heat to medium-low and cook until the whites are fully set, 2 to 3 minutes. If there's still a little uncooked egg on top, flick a few drops of water into the skillet and cover, steaming the eggs just until the whites are fully set, about 20 seconds.

BIBIMBAP WITH MUSHROOMS AND ZUCCHINI

SERVES 4

Bibimbap is a Korean rice dish that's infinitely variable, as it can be topped with many kinds of vegetables and sometimes meat. The constants for this dish: warm rice, a few different vegetables (which are usually cooked or pickled), and gochujang, the sweet-and-spicy Korean chili paste. Traditionally, bibimbap is made with white short-grain rice, but black rice and red rice are especially delicious too.

Typically, everything is arranged over the rice and mixed at the table. Most bibimbap, including this one, is also topped with a fried egg, which, when stirred in, acts as a sauce that you can mix with gochujang at the table.

FOR THE MARINATED VEGETABLES	FOR THE COOKED VEGETABLES		FOR SERVING	CONT'D
1 Tbsp unseasoned rice vinegar	3 Tbsp canola oil	2 medium zucchini, halved lengthwise and sliced about ¼ in [6 mm] thick	1 Tbsp canola oil	
1 tsp sugar	8 oz [230 g] shiitake mushrooms, stems discarded (or saved for stock), caps halved or quartered if large	1 garlic clove, thinly sliced	4 large eggs	
¼ tsp salt			Salt	
1 cup [about 140 g] thinly sliced or julienned crisp vegetables, such as radishes, carrots, cauliflower, or cucumbers		4 tsp soy sauce	4 to 5 cups [480 to 600 g] hot cooked rice (see page 48)	
	Salt	½ tsp sugar	Sliced green onions, for garnish	
		One 5 oz [140 g] bag baby spinach	Gochujang, thinned with water if desired, for serving	
		½ tsp toasted sesame oil		

TO MAKE THE MARINATED VEGETABLES, in a medium bowl, stir together the vinegar, sugar, and salt. Add the vegetables and toss; let stand while you prepare the rest of the bibimbap.

TO MAKE THE COOKED VEGETABLES, in a large, well-seasoned cast-iron or nonstick skillet over medium-high heat, warm 1½ Tbsp of the oil. Add the shiitake mushrooms, season with salt, and cook, stirring, until starting to soften, about 3 minutes. Add the remaining 1½ Tbsp of oil and the zucchini and season with salt. Cook, stirring, until the zucchini starts to soften and the mushrooms are browned, about 2 minutes. Add the garlic and cook, stirring, until softened, about 2 minutes. Add the soy sauce and sugar and stir until completely incorporated and the soy sauce is absorbed. Taste and season with more salt as desired. Scrape the vegetables into one side of a bowl.

Add the spinach and a few drops of water to the skillet and cook, stirring, until wilted, about 2 minutes. Season with salt. Remove from the heat and stir in the sesame oil, then transfer the spinach to the other side of the bowl.

TO FINISH AND SERVE, in the same skillet over medium heat, warm the oil. Crack the eggs in the skillet and cook until the bottoms are set, about 2 minutes. Lower the heat to medium-low and cook until the egg whites are fully set but the yolks are still runny, 2 to 3 minutes. (For more about cooking sunny-side up eggs, see page 77.)

Spoon the rice into bowls. Arrange the marinated vegetables, mushrooms and zucchini, and spinach in separate piles over the rice. Set an egg on top and sprinkle with salt. Garnish with green onions and serve with gochujang, allowing everyone to mix it in to their liking.

CHEESY RICE PATTIES WITH POACHED EGGS AND SPINACH

SERVES 2 TO 4

Leftover rice, meet brunch. Rice patties are a tastier (and gluten-free) alternative to the ubiquitous English muffin. Because the cheese and green onions in the patties bring so much richness and flavor, you really don't need any hollandaise. A little hot sauce, however, doesn't hurt. Don't worry if the patties don't form perfect rounds; those stray edges become delightfully browned and crispy.

Poaching eggs can feel a little bit intimidating, but it doesn't have to be. Just know that when you poach eggs, there is almost always some wispy bits of egg white left in the pot; it's not a sign of failure. Fresh eggs hold together best when poached. If you're unsure about their freshness, you can crack the eggs one by one into a fine-mesh sieve before poaching to allow the most liquid part of the egg whites to drip through. This will ensure you have tidy poached eggs.

6 large eggs

1½ cups [180 g] cooked short- or medium-grain white or brown rice (see page 48), cooled slightly or chilled

2 green onions, thinly sliced

3 oz [85 g] Cheddar cheese, grated

½ tsp salt, plus more for sprinkling

2 Tbsp extra-virgin olive oil

One 5 oz [140 g] bag baby spinach or arugula

Hot sauce, for serving (optional)

In a large bowl, beat together 2 of the eggs. Add the rice, green onions, Cheddar, and salt and stir until incorporated.

Bring a large saucepan of water to a bare simmer. Crack 2 of the remaining eggs into small bowls or ramekins. Using a spoon, swirl the water gently to create a vortex and slip the eggs one by one into the water. Don't worry if there are stray egg white pieces in the water; most of the egg white should wrap around the egg yolk. Let the eggs poach until the whites are set but the yolks are still runny, about 3 minutes, keeping the water hot but not bubbling. Using a slotted spoon, transfer the eggs to a bowl. Use the spoon to remove and discard any stray egg white, then repeat with the remaining 2 eggs.

CONT'D

Meanwhile, in a large nonstick skillet over
medium-high heat, warm the oil. When the
oil is hot enough that a grain of rice sizzles
when added to the skillet, use a ½ cup [120 ml]
measure to scoop four mounds of the rice
mixture into the skillet. Cook, pressing them
gently with a spatula so they're about ½ in
[13 mm] thick, until the bottoms are deeply
golden, 2 to 3 minutes. Flip and cook until the
second sides are nicely browned, then transfer
to four plates.

Add the spinach and a few drops of water to
the skillet and cook, stirring, until wilted, 1 to
2 minutes. Season with salt. Pile the spinach
on top of the cakes and top each cake with a
poached egg. Sprinkle the eggs with a little salt
and serve with hot sauce, if desired.

SAVORY RICE TORTA

SERVES 4 TO 6

In northern Italy, you find sweet or savory dishes known as torta del riso. Sometimes, the tortas have a flour-based crust. Other times, they are crustless, like this one. Much like a frittata, this torta tastes best at room temperature and keeps well overnight. You can also vary the vegetable fillings based on what you have on hand.

2 Tbsp butter, plus more for the pan

1 oz [30 g] Parmigiano-Reggiano cheese, finely grated

2 cups [480 ml] whole milk

½ cup [100 g] arborio rice

Salt

1 small yellow onion, chopped

Freshly ground pepper (preferably white pepper)

One 5 oz [140 g] bag baby arugula or spinach

6 large eggs

4 oz [115 g] Gruyère cheese, grated

Preheat the oven to 350°F [180°C] and butter a 9 in [23 cm] cake pan. Sprinkle the Parmigiano-Reggiano cheese in the bottom of the cake pan and tip the pan so it sticks to the sides of the pan as well. Set the cake pan on a baking sheet.

In a small saucepan over medium heat, combine 1 cup [240 ml] of the milk with the rice and a few large pinches of salt and bring to a simmer, stirring. Remove from the heat and let cool until just warm.

In a medium skillet over medium heat, melt the butter. Add the onion, season generously with salt and pepper, and cook, stirring, until softened, about 8 minutes. Add the arugula in batches and cook, stirring, until wilted, about 1 minute. Remove from the heat and let cool to warm. Season with more salt, if desired.

In a bowl, whisk together the eggs. Add the remaining 1 cup [240 ml] of milk followed by the warm rice-milk mixture and whisk together. Stir in the cooked vegetables and the Gruyère cheese. Pour the mixture into the prepared pan, then bake on the baking sheet until golden, puffed, and completely set in the center, 45 to 50 minutes.

Carefully transfer the pan to a wire rack and let the torta cool to room temperature. Run a butter knife around the edge of the pan to loosen. Invert the pan to flip out the torta onto a plate or serve in wedges right from the pan.

MAKE AHEAD The torta can be assembled up to 1 day ahead and refrigerated overnight, then baked. The baked torta can be refrigerated for up to 1 day. Bring to room temperature before serving.

RAMEN "CARBONARA" WITH CORN

SERVES 4

Comforting and crowd-pleasing, this dish is great for breakfast or really any time of day. Corn is hardly traditional in pasta alla carbonara, but it melds so well with bacon, eggs, and cheese, we wonder if the Italians who created the dish might have added sweet corn had it been available to them.

Salt

1 large egg plus 2 large egg yolks

¼ cup [8 g] grated Parmigiano-Reggiano cheese

8 oz [230 g] sliced bacon, thinly sliced crosswise

2 large or 3 medium ears of corn, kernels removed from the cob, or 1½ cup [210 g] thawed frozen corn

Freshly ground pepper

10 oz [280 g] Lotus Foods rice ramen noodles, such as brown rice and millet, or other ramen noodles

Snipped chives or thinly sliced green onion tops

Bring a large soup pot of generously salted water to a boil.

In a large bowl, whisk together the eggs, yolks, and cheese.

In a large skillet over medium-low heat, add the bacon and cook, stirring occasionally, until just crisp, 10 to 15 minutes. Using a slotted spoon, transfer the bacon to a paper towel–lined plate. Drain off all but 1 Tbsp of the fat from the skillet, then add the corn and 1 to 2 Tbsp of water. Cook, scraping up any browned bits, until just hot, 1 to 2 minutes. Season the corn with salt and pepper and remove from the heat.

Add the noodles to the boiling water and cook for 1 minute, then use a fork to separate and cook for 3 more minutes, until just cooked. Scoop out ½ cup [120 ml] of the cooking water, then drain the noodles.

Add the noodles, corn, and reserved cooking water to the egg mixture and toss. Taste and season with salt and pepper. Transfer to bowls and garnish with the bacon and chives.

2

SNACKS
AND SOUPS

RICE IS LIFE

More than half the world's people rely on rice for their daily meals, and white rice—milled to remove the fiber-rich bran layer—is the most popular. Most Western nutritionists tend to view white rice, unless enriched with additional vitamins, as little more than a gluten-free source of carbohydrates with a small amount of protein. They tout whole-grain rice varieties for their higher nutrient content, and for good reason. Whole-grain rice varieties—which includes brown, red, and black rice—contain significantly more fiber as well as more protein, fat, vitamin B_6, vitamin E, and minerals like manganese and magnesium compared to white rice. The fatty acids in rice bran are 80 percent polyunsaturated. High levels of polyunsaturated fatty compounds are effective in lowering blood cholesterol levels. Whole-grain rice also has a lower glycemic index because the fiber in the rice is digested more slowly than the simple carbohydrates in white rice, which break down faster into sugar.

Pigmented varieties of rice, including the many shades of black and red rice, are especially nutritious because their colorful bran layers contain phytonutrients known as anthocyanins, which you'll also find in foods like berries, cherries, and red cabbage. Research shows that anthocyanins have antioxidant, anti-inflammatory, and anti-cancer effects. A comparison of the antioxidant capacity in black and red rice with that in corn, oats, and red and white wheat found that it was 2 to 4.5 times higher in pigmented rice. The consumption of anthocyanins in the United States is thought to be only 12.5 mg per day per person. In a USDA study, the concentration of total anthocyanins in 100 g of cooked black rice was 170 mg, while the concentration in an equal amount of fresh blueberries was 124 mg. This led the researchers to conclude that "darker color bran whole-grain rices have potential to positively impact human health." Other research has found links between lowered serum triglyceride levels in black and red rice, and one study showed that the anthocyanins from black rice stopped the growth of breast cancer cells in test tubes. Even if we don't yet fully understand the effects of all these micronutrients in the body, it's clear that black and red rice are nutritional superstars.

In Eastern nutritional philosophy, rice is appreciated for more than its macro- and micronutrient content. Rice is thought about in spiritual terms and often seen as a source of life force. It's valued for the ways it is thought to affect the body's systems. For example, practitioners of both traditional Chinese medicine and Ayurveda view rice as a food to help keep the body in balance and appreciate white rice because it's easy to digest. In China, doctors and other healers sometimes prescribe black and red rice as a supplement to strengthen the blood and support the kidneys and liver when people need it.

While studies show that, yes, whole-grain varieties of rice are undoubtably "healthier," don't discount the digestibility of white rice. If you have a condition that affects the gut, like Crohn's disease or irritable bowel syndrome; a short-term gastrointestinal illness; or just want to give your digestive system a short break, white rice can be a great food choice. (Of course, always talk to your doctor or dietician when in need of a special diet.)

So . . . which rice is the "best" choice? We say—if you are able to eat a varied diet, then choose whatever is most delicious with what you're eating and makes the most sense for you. To be honest, we don't obsess about the nutrients in each individual variety of rice too much. Instead, we like to mix up the varieties we eat and include white rice in the mix, especially when our plates are packed with lots of good-for-us vegetables. We hope the recipes in this book help you see just how diverse and delicious rice can be!

FURIKAKE RICE BALLS

**SERVES
4**

In Japan and Korea, you often find simple snacks made with seasoned rice and sometimes cooked vegetables or meats tucked into lunch boxes or picnic baskets. This version uses furikake, a seasoning blend that varies from brand to brand but typically contains sesame seeds and nori seaweed. If you have leftover warm short-grain rice from your meal, these take a mere five minutes to pull together.

2 cups [360 g] cooked warm Jade Pearl Rice™ or other short-grain rice (see page 48)

1½ to 2 tsp soy sauce

½ tsp toasted sesame oil

3 Tbsp furikake

In a mixing bowl, place the cooked rice and, using a wooden spoon or rice paddle, stir the soy sauce and sesame oil into the rice until incorporated. Add the furikake and stir to incorporate. Taste and add more soy sauce, if desired.

Using lightly moistened hands, form the rice into twelve balls and serve.

MAKE AHEAD The rice balls can be refrigerated overnight. Bring to room temperature before serving.

**USING
LEFTOVER
RICE**

In her book *The Seventh Daughter*, Cecilia Chiang wrote that her mother would say that each grain of rice represents one worker's drop of sweat, so rice must never be wasted. Every rice culture has a way to use up and extend leftover rice into a delicious snack or new meal, from fried rice (see page 71) to rice balls (see above) to rice patties or cakes (see pages 81 and 95). We love these kinds of dishes so much that we often make extra rice just so we have it on hand.

SCALLION RICE CAKES WITH DIPPING SAUCE

SERVES 4 TO 6

There's no beating a good scallion pancake, with its layered, flaky dough. But these lacy, crispy rice cakes will scratch the itch if you're craving those flavors. They're also an easy way to use up any leftover rice you might have on hand, but they're so good, you might want to cook some rice just to make them!

When you first stir together the rice mixture, it might seem like it won't hold together, but they will with the magic of a little heat.

FOR THE DIPPING SAUCE

¾ tsp sugar

1½ tsp warm water

2 Tbsp soy sauce

2 Tbsp unseasoned rice vinegar

1 tsp chili-garlic sauce or sambal ulek

FOR THE CAKES

2 cups [360 g] cooked short-to-medium-grain white or brown rice (see page 48)

2 large eggs, lightly beaten

8 green onions, thinly sliced

1 tsp toasted sesame oil

¾ tsp fine sea salt

Vegetable oil, for cooking

TO MAKE THE DIPPING SAUCE, in a bowl, dissolve the sugar in the water. Stir in the soy sauce, rice vinegar, and chili-garlic sauce.

TO MAKE THE CAKES, in a large bowl, gently mix together the rice, eggs, green onions, sesame oil, and salt. Line a plate with paper towels.

In a large nonstick or well-seasoned cast-iron skillet over medium-high heat, warm about ⅛ in [3 mm] of oil until it's hot enough that a grain of rice sizzles when it touches the oil. For each cake, use a ¼ cup [60 ml] measure to scoop enough of the rice mixture so it's about three-quarters full and add the mixture to the skillet. Use a spatula to press into thin patties; don't worry if they are not perfect rounds. Cook until nicely golden on the bottom, about 2 minutes, then flip. Cook until golden on the second side, 1 to 2 minutes longer. Lower the heat if the oil starts to smoke or the patties brown too fast. Transfer the patties to the plate and repeat with the remaining rice mixture, adding more oil as necessary. Serve with the dipping sauce.

GRILLED STICKY RICE SKEWERS WITH PEANUT SAUCE

SERVES 4

This recipe is inspired by khao jee, a popular street-food dish in the Isan region of Thailand, where a group of farmers grows organic rice we import. Also known as glutinous or sweet rice, sticky rice is high in amylopectin starch, which makes it appealingly sticky and chewy. To prevent sticky rice from turning to mush, it's typically soaked for several hours and then steamed, which is what we do here.

After the rice is steamed, it's then grilled to form a crisp crust and served with a lightly sweet and savory peanut sauce. This recipe makes more of the peanut sauce than you need, but it's a great condiment to have on hand for tossing with noodles or serving with vegetables. You will need eight skewers to make this recipe.

FOR THE PEANUT SAUCE

¼ cup [60 ml] coconut milk

¼ cup [65 g] peanut butter

1 to 2 Tbsp soy sauce

1 to 2 Tbsp honey

1 tsp chili-garlic sauce or sambal ulek

FOR THE RICE SKEWERS

1 cup [200 g] white sticky rice, rinsed, then soaked 8 to 12 hours

Oil, for the grill

Salt

1 large egg, lightly beaten

TO MAKE THE PEANUT SAUCE, in a bowl, whisk together the coconut milk, peanut butter, soy sauce, honey, and chili-garlic sauce. Add 2 Tbsp of water, then taste and add more water as desired to thin out the mixture. Set aside.

TO MAKE THE RICE SKEWERS, in a strainer, drain the soaked rice.

Line a steamer basket or fine-mesh sieve with cheesecloth so it overhangs the edge and transfer the rice to it. Fill a soup pot that holds the steamer basket or sieve with about 1 in [2.5 cm] of water. Set the rice in the steamer basket over the water, cover, and bring to a boil. When the water boils, steam the rice for

CONT'D

15 minutes. Remove the rice from the steamer basket and use the overhang of the cheesecloth to carefully flip the solid disk of sticky rice onto a plate. Return the cheesecloth to the basket and the rice to the cheesecloth so the cooked side is now up, then return to the pot. Steam the rice until cooked through but not mushy, about 15 minutes longer.

Remove the rice from the heat, uncover, and let cool until just warm. As the rice cools, soak 8 thin wooden skewers in cool water.

Preheat a grill or grill pan over medium-high heat and lightly coat the grates with oil. Using damp hands, break the warm sticky rice into eight chunks (each about ¼ cup [90 g]) and form them into cylinders about 3 in [7.5 cm] long and 1 in [2.5 cm] thick. Thread the cylinders onto the skewers and season lightly with salt.

Grill the rice, turning occasionally, until some of the kernels start to brown, about 2 minutes. Brush the rice with the egg and cook, turning, until golden and crisp, 30 seconds to 1 minute.

Transfer the sticky rice skewers to a platter and serve with the peanut sauce.

VEGETABLE TEMAKI
(HAND-ROLLED SUSHI)

SERVES 8 AS A SNACK

Making sushi at home can feel a bit intimidating or fussy, and the truth is, many people in Japan eat sushi only when they go out. Hand-rolled sushi, however, known as temaki, is more popular at home. Temaki starts with seasoned rice—we love using our Jade Pearl Rice™, but any short-grained rice for sushi will do. For the fillings, you can choose your own adventure. We highly recommend something pickled and these umami-rich mushrooms. We have included a list of raw vegetables and herbs you can try.

FOR THE QUICK PICKLES	FOR THE RICE	FOR THE MUSHROOMS	FOR SERVING	CONT'D
1 Tbsp unseasoned rice vinegar	3 Tbsp unseasoned rice vinegar	¼ cup [60 ml] soy sauce	One small package nori sheets, each sheet cut in half	
1 tsp sugar	2 tsp sugar	2 Tbsp mirin		
¼ tsp salt	½ tsp salt	½ tsp smoked paprika	Optional additional fillings:	
1 cup [about 140 g] sliced fruit or vegetables of your choice, such as peeled apples, peeled firm peaches or plums, cucumbers, kohlrabi, turnips, or radishes	One 3 in [7.5 cm] piece kombu (optional)	1 lb [455 g] shiitake mushrooms, stems removed, caps cut into ½ in [13 mm] strips	Sliced avocado	
	1 cup [200 g] cooked and warm Jade Pearl Rice™ or sushi rice (see page 48)		Microgreens	
		Vegetable oil	Thinly sliced green onion	
			Small shiso leaves	
			Sliced radish	
			Julienned carrot	
			Julienned cucumber	

The easiest way to build temaki is to take a halved sheet of nori and hold one side in the palm of your hand. (Make sure your hands are dry first!) Fill that side with about 2 Tbsp of rice and press it so it forms a diagonal bed. (If you're holding the seaweed in your left hand, leave the bottom left corner free of rice; reverse that if you're holding it in your right hand.) Arrange any fillings on top of the bed of rice on the same diagonal. Fold the empty corner of the nori up and over the filling toward the center of the nori. Continue rolling the nori around the filling to form a cone. If you would like the cone to hold together, you can take a grain of rice and use it as glue. But temaki is also delicious when folded and eaten quickly.

TO MAKE THE QUICK PICKLES, in a bowl, whisk together the vinegar, sugar, and salt. Add the sliced fruit or vegetables and let stand while you prepare the rest of the components.

TO MAKE THE RICE, in a bowl or jar, combine the vinegar, sugar, and salt until the salt and sugar dissolve. Add the kombu, if using, and let stand for 15 minutes. Remove the kombu from the vinegar, then add the vinegar mixture to the warm rice and let stand for about 10 minutes.

TO MAKE THE MUSHROOMS, in a large bowl, combine the soy sauce, mirin, and smoked paprika. Add the sliced mushrooms and toss. Let stand for at least 5 minutes.

When you're nearly ready to serve, heat 1 Tbsp of oil in a large skillet over medium-high heat and add the mushrooms with their liquid. Cook, stirring frequently, until the mushrooms wilt and start to brown in spots, 3 to 5 minutes. Scrape into a bowl.

TO SERVE, set out the halved pieces of nori with the rice, mushrooms, quick pickles, and remaining fillings. Serve, allowing people to assemble their own temaki. (See Note.)

BROCCOLI BISQUE

This is the soup to make when you have just a handful of white rice left in the pantry. The rice acts as a thickener and gives the soup a creamy texture. The Parmesan rind, coriander seeds, and lemon zest make the soup taste greater than the sum of its parts, and adding leafy greens at the end brightens its color.

2 broccoli stalks, 8 oz [230 g] each

2 Tbsp extra-virgin olive oil

1 large yellow onion, roughly chopped

2 garlic cloves, smashed

Salt

1 tsp coriander seeds

½ cup [100 g] white jasmine rice or other white rice

1 Parmesan cheese rind or ¼ cup [8 g] freshly grated Parmigiano-Reggiano cheese

2 packed cups [40 g] arugula or tender mustard greens

Finely grated zest of 1 lemon

Freshly ground pepper

Separate the stalks from the crowns of the broccoli. Using a large knife, peel off the tough skin of the stalk and roughly chop the inner core. Pull the broccoli crowns into small florets.

In a large soup pot over medium heat, heat the olive oil. Add the onion and garlic and season generously with salt; cook, stirring occasionally, until the onion is softened, about 8 minutes. Add the broccoli, season with salt, and cook, stirring, until bright green, about 2 minutes. Add the coriander seeds and cook until fragrant, about 30 seconds. Add 6 cups [1.4 L] of water, the rice, and the Parmigiano-Reggiano rind, increase the heat to high, and bring to a boil. Lower the heat to medium-low and simmer until the rice and broccoli are very tender, 15 to 20 minutes.

Turn off the heat, remove the Parmesan rind, and stir in the arugula until wilted. Stir in the lemon zest.

Using an immersion blender, purée the soup. Alternatively, let the soup cool until just warm and ladle it into a blender—in batches if necessary—and purée. Taste the soup, season with salt and pepper, and serve hot.

KHICHDI WITH CARROTS AND SPINACH

SERVES 2 TO 4

Khichdi is a popular dish across India that brings together rice and legumes in one pot. It's often made with hulled mung beans, known as moong dal, which add a sunny yellow color to the dish. While khichdi can be served any time of day for any reason, it's especially good when you're seeking something soothing and easy to digest. Feel free to play around with adding different types of vegetables to make this dish your own.

Yogurt and spicy-salty Indian mango or lime pickles are great accompaniments, but this is also delicious without them. For an even richer tasting and more flavorful khichdi, toast cumin seeds and mustard seeds in ghee and then drizzle on top just before serving.

1 Tbsp ghee plus 1 Tbsp for serving (optional)

½ tsp cumin seeds

½ tsp coriander seeds

½ tsp fennel seeds

¼ tsp ground turmeric

Freshly ground pepper

1 medium carrot, grated

Salt

½ cup [100 g] white basmati rice

½ cup [100 g] hulled yellow mung beans (moong dal) or red lentils

8 oz [230 g] mature spinach, leaves torn

Cilantro leaves, for garnish

Yogurt and Indian mango or lime pickles, for serving (optional)

In a large saucepan over medium heat, warm 1 Tbsp of the ghee. Add the cumin, coriander, and fennel seeds and toast just until fragrant, about 30 seconds. Add the turmeric and a few grinds of pepper and toast for 10 seconds. Add the carrot, season with salt, and cook, stirring, until just softened, about 2 minutes. Stir in the rice and mung beans, then add 1 qt [960 ml] of water and bring to a boil over high heat. Lower the heat to medium-low, cover partially, and cook until the rice and moong dal are tender and porridgey, 18 to 23 minutes. Add the spinach and cover the saucepan. Cook until the spinach is wilted, about 5 minutes. Stir the spinach into the khichdi and season with more salt as desired. Add 1 more Tbsp of ghee if you'd like a richer-tasting khichdi.

Transfer the khichdi to bowls and garnish with cilantro. Serve with yogurt and mango or lime pickle, if desired.

SPRING MINESTRONE WITH WHITE BEANS AND BLACK RICE

SERVES 4

This easy soup is just the thing to make when the first asparagus pokes through the earth and the nights are still cool. Because it's so simple, use the best-quality broth you can find. The soup is fairly chunky; if you'd like more broth, by all means, add some. If you'd like a little more richness, drizzle with more olive oil and sprinkle with Parmesan cheese.

¼ cup [60 ml] extra-virgin olive oil

1 leek, white and light green parts only, thinly sliced into rings and rinsed well (save the leek tops for stock)

Salt

1 qt [960 ml] low-sodium chicken or vegetable broth

½ cup [100 g] Forbidden Rice® or other non-sticky black rice

One 15 oz [430 g] can white beans with liquid

1 lb [455 g] asparagus, trimmed and cut into 1 in [2.5 cm] pieces

1 cup [120 g] frozen peas

Torn basil or mint, for garnish

In a large soup pot or Dutch oven over medium heat, warm the olive oil. Add the leek, season with salt, and cook until softened, about 4 minutes. Add the broth and rice, increase the heat to medium-high, and bring to a boil, then lower the heat to medium and simmer until the rice is al dente, about 20 minutes. Add the white beans with their liquid and stir to heat through. Add the asparagus and peas and cook until bright green and heated through, about 1 minute. Season the soup with more salt as desired.

Ladle the soup into bowls, garnish with basil or mint, and serve.

MISO BROTH WITH SWEET POTATOES, BOK CHOY, AND RAMEN

SERVES 4

This soup tastes indulgent because of the sweet potatoes and miso but is also incredibly nourishing. You can use the rice ramen noodles we make at Lotus Foods or other dried ramen noodles.

7 oz [200 g] firm tofu, cut into ½ in [13 mm] cubes

1 Tbsp soy sauce

4 rice ramen noodle cakes (about 10 oz [280 g] total)

2 Tbsp canola oil

1 tsp finely grated fresh ginger (from 1 in [2.5 cm] peeled ginger)

2 garlic cloves, finely grated

2 medium sweet potatoes, peeled and cut into ½ in [13 mm] pieces

Salt

1 qt [960 ml] low-sodium chicken or vegetable broth

2 heads baby bok choy, ribs separated from the leaves and washed, ribs chopped, leaves torn

⅓ cup [85 g] white miso

Juice of 1 lemon

Shichimi togarashi (Japanese seven-spice blend), for serving (optional)

In a small bowl, toss the tofu with the soy sauce and let stand while you prepare the soup.

In a large soup pot of boiling salted water, cook the noodles until just tender, about 5 minutes. Drain and rinse under cold water.

In the same pot over medium heat, warm the oil. Add the ginger and garlic and cook until fragrant, 1 minute. Add the sweet potatoes, season lightly with salt, and stir to coat with the aromatics. Add the broth and 2 cups [480 ml] of water and bring to a boil over high heat. Lower the heat and simmer until the sweet potatoes are just tender, 8 to 12 minutes. Add the marinated tofu and cook for 1 minute. Add the ribs of the bok choy and stir to wilt.

Ladle about 1 cup [240 ml] of broth into a bowl. Whisk in the miso and lemon juice, then return the broth to the pot. Season with more salt, if desired. Keep warm over low heat.

Rinse the noodles under warm water, drain well, and transfer them to bowls. Divide the bok choy leaves among the bowls, then ladle the hot soup on top. Serve with shichimi togarashi, if desired.

SOBA NOODLES WITH GREEN TEA BROTH AND SMOKED SALMON

SERVES 2 TO 4

This dish is inspired by ochazuke, a Japanese dish that is usually made with steamed rice in a simple broth of green tea or dashi. In this recipe, we use soba noodles instead because they taste especially nice with the green tea.

You can add many different toppings to ochazuke, from grilled or raw fish, fish roe, grilled meats, pickled vegetables, or umeboshi (Japanese pickled plums). Here, we suggest storebought hot-smoked salmon because it adds so much flavor and requires no extra cooking. You can find hot-smoked salmon in the seafood section of many grocery stores. Instead of looking glossy like lox, it resembles a cooked fillet of salmon.

8 oz [230 g] rice-soba or other soba noodles

3 green tea or genmaicha tea bags or 3 tsp loose-leaf green tea or genmaicha

8 oz [230 g] hot-smoked salmon, skin removed

Sliced green onions, soy sauce, and furikake seasoning, for serving (optional)

In a large soup pot of boiling salted water, cook the noodles according to the package directions until al dente. Drain and rinse under warm water.

Meanwhile, bring a kettle of water to a boil. Measure out 3 cups [720 ml] of the water and steep the tea in it for 3 minutes, then remove the tea bags or strain the tea.

Using tongs, transfer the noodles to bowls. (Rinse them again under hot water first if they are sticking.)

Flake apart the fish and divide it among the bowls.

Pour the tea over the noodles and fish and serve, adding green onions, soy sauce, and furikake, as desired.

AVGOLEMONO SOUP WITH RICE AND SMOKED FISH

SERVES 2 TO 4

Avgolemono is a broth that's thickened with a combination of lemon juice and egg. It's popular in Greek cooking, but you can find it in other parts of the Mediterranean as well. The goal is to add the egg at the end of cooking, warming it enough so it turns the broth silky but doesn't scramble. White rice acts as an additional thickener in this soup.

2 Tbsp extra-virgin olive oil

1 medium yellow onion, chopped

Salt

½ cup [100 g] medium- or long-grain white rice, such as jasmine or basmati

1 qt [960 ml] low-sodium chicken or vegetable broth

4 to 5 oz [115 to 140 g] smoked trout or mackerel, skin removed and flesh broken into large flakes

2 Tbsp fresh lemon juice

2 large eggs

¼ cup [10 g] chopped dill, for garnish

In a medium saucepan over medium heat, warm the olive oil. Add the onion, season with salt, and cook until translucent, about 8 minutes. Add the rice, broth, and 1 cup [240 ml] of water and cook until the rice is tender, about 15 minutes.

Add the trout to the soup and cook until heated through, about 2 minutes. Lower the heat to low.

In a mixing bowl, whisk together the lemon juice and eggs. Carefully ladle about 1 cup [240 ml] of the soup into the eggs while whisking constantly. Carefully add the egg mixture to the soup, stirring constantly. As soon as the soup looks thickened, remove it from the heat.

Ladle the soup into bowls, sprinkle with the dill, and serve.

RICE SOUP WITH CLAMS
AND LEMONGRASS BROTH

**SERVES
4**

In this southern Vietnamese–inspired dish, we steam clams in a fragrant ginger and lemongrass broth and then use that liquid to make the soup, adding rice to the liquid to thicken the broth.

Rau răm, which is used as a bright garnish, is sometimes called Vietnamese coriander. It has a flavor that's a little bit like cilantro but more intense. You can grow it in your herb garden or find it at some Southeast Asian markets. Or you can substitute cilantro.

1 stalk lemongrass

2 Tbsp canola oil

1 Tbsp finely grated fresh ginger (from 3 in [7.5 cm] peeled ginger)

5 garlic cloves, finely grated

1 Tbsp fish sauce

4 dozen littleneck clams, scrubbed of grit, broken ones discarded

2 cups [240 g] cooked jasmine rice

Salt (optional)

Rau răm leaves or cilantro leaves, lime wedges, and freshly ground pepper, for serving

Chop off the top 4 in [10 cm] and the bottom of the lemongrass. Remove the tough outer pieces and save them to make tea or stock, if desired. Finely chop the tender inner core.

In a large, heavy soup pot or Dutch oven with a tight-fitting lid over medium heat, warm the oil. Add the lemongrass, ginger, and garlic and cook, stirring, until fragrant and the aromatics start sticking to the pot. Add 1 cup [240 ml] of water and the fish sauce and bring to a simmer. Add the clams, cover, and cook for 4 minutes. Uncover and, using a slotted spoon, transfer any open clams to a large bowl. Continue cooking, maintaining the heat so the liquid simmers and stirring occasionally; remove the clams as they open. If there are any stubborn clams that are not opening, cover the pot once more for 1 minute. Discard any clams that refuse to open.

CONT'D

Carefully strain the liquid through a very fine-mesh sieve or a cheesecloth-lined strainer into a measuring cup, then wipe out the pan to remove any grit.

In the same pot, combine the clam liquid with enough water to total 6 cups [1.5 L] of liquid. Add the rice and bring to a boil over medium-high heat, stirring occasionally to make sure the rice doesn't stick to the bottom of the pot. Lower the heat to medium and simmer, stirring occasionally and being sure to scrape the bottom of the pot, until the rice is very soft and its starch starts to thicken the broth, about 15 minutes. When you're nearly ready to serve, taste and season with salt, if desired, remembering the salty clams will be added to the soup.

Add the clams to the soup (you can shuck them first if you'd like), cover the pot and cook for 1 minute, until the clams are hot. Ladle the clams and soup into bowls. Tear rau răm leaves and sprinkle on top, then serve with lime wedges and pepper.

CREAMY CHICKEN AND RED RICE SOUP

SERVES 4

The most famous rice grown in France is from Camargue along the Mediterranean, and it's almost always red. This chicken and red rice soup looks to France for inspiration, combining classic aromatics known as mirepoix (onion, carrot, and celery) with herbes de Provence and a touch of cream. Herbes de Provence is a dried herb blend that can vary from brand to brand and cook to cook but usually includes herbs like thyme, basil, rosemary, tarragon, savory, and sometimes lavender. If you purchase it just to make this soup, you'll find yourself using it as a rub for chicken or to toss with roasted vegetables. While you can simply substitute dried thyme for the herbes de Provence, the flavor of the soup won't be as complex. If you'd like a brighter flavor in the soup, add a squeeze of lemon juice at the end.

2 chicken breast halves (1 to 1¼ lb [455 to 570 g])

Salt

¼ cup [60 ml] extra-virgin olive oil

1 large yellow onion, chopped

1 large carrot, chopped

1 celery rib, chopped

1 lb [455 g] button or cremini mushrooms, wiped clean, trimmed, and thinly sliced

Freshly ground pepper

½ tsp herbes de Provence

½ cup [120 ml] dry white wine

6 cups [1.4 L] chicken stock

1 small bunch Tuscan kale, stems removed, leaves coarsely chopped

3 cups [360 g] cooked red rice (see page 48)

½ cup [120 ml] heavy cream

Trim any fat from the chicken and cut it into 1 in [2.5 cm] pieces. In a large bowl, toss the chicken with a few generous pinches of salt and let stand while you prepare the soup.

In a Dutch oven over medium heat, warm the olive oil. Add the onion, carrot, celery, and mushrooms, season generously with salt and lightly with pepper, and cook, stirring frequently, until the vegetables are softened, about 15 minutes. Add the herbes de Provence and cook until fragrant, about 30 seconds. Add the white wine and cook, stirring, until evaporated. Add the chicken, stock, and kale and bring to a boil. Lower the heat to a simmer and cook until the chicken is cooked through and the kale is tender, 10 to 15 minutes. Stir in the rice and cream and cook just until hot, 1 minute. Season the soup with more salt and pepper, if desired, and serve.

3

SALADS AND SIDES

AN UNEXPECTED BENEFIT OF SRI: IMPROVING WOMEN'S LIVES

Women are the unsung heroes of rice production. Researchers estimate that over half a billion women and girls work on family farms or as wage laborers in rice fields and that they contribute 80 percent of the labor to grow rice globally. If true, this means there are more women engaged in producing rice than any other single livelihood!

So, what is it that women do? While men typically prep the land, apply agrochemicals, and assist with harvesting, it is women who usually do the truly back-breaking repetitive tasks. These include sowing the seed nurseries, uprooting seedlings for transplanting, transporting seedlings to the main fields, transplanting the seedlings, weeding and harvesting the fields, and cleaning, threshing, and drying the rice. They often do all this work with no tools other than their hands and a small scythe.

In traditional rice production, women carry out these tasks for weeks and months at a time in flooded fields, where their hands and legs are constantly immersed in stagnant water that is often infested with leeches and other disease vectors, like mosquitos, which can cause malaria. These conditions can lead to both acute and chronic health problems. As men increasingly head to cities and towns to supplement family incomes with off-farm work, women now sometimes apply the fertilizers and pesticides as well—a particularly concerning trend because pesticides absorb more readily into women's bodies and can even affect their unborn children.

When farmers switch to System of Rice Intensification (see SRI, page 55) growing methods, women report numerous benefits. It sounds counterintuitive, but to get the higher yields, they use 80 to 90 percent fewer seedlings. With fewer seedlings to manage, they can do the work early in the day or late afternoon when the sun isn't as hot. SRI seedlings are also significantly lighter. Under conventional practices, for one acre, they transplant as many as 2,600 lb [1,180 kg] worth of seedlings in bundles weighing between 15 to 66 lb [7 to 30 kg]. Using SRI practices, for that same acre, women might carry only 320 lb [145 kg] of seedlings in bundles weighing between 11 and 13 lb [5 and 6 kg].

By producing more rice from less land, families can free up part of their farmland to cultivate fruits and vegetables and even dig ponds to store water and cultivate fish.

A simple rotary weeder—a luxury for many smallholder farmers—enables women to weed the fields much faster, and they work in an upright rather than bent-over posture. In many regions, using a mechanical tool is considered a task for men, so women are freed up from the weeding altogether.

With less time spent transplanting seedlings and weeding, these women have more time to cook, take care of their children, start a business, or just relax. Perhaps most important, because they no longer work constantly in standing water, they experience fewer skin and gynecological issues and less exposure to disease vectors like mosquitos. And they have less chronic neck and back pain from spending so many hours working bent over. We believe that when we consider better, more ecological ways of growing rice, we must consider the people who grow it.

WOMEN'S WORK: COMPARING CONVENTIONAL AND SRI GROWING PRACTICES IN ODISHA, INDIA

	CONVENTIONAL PRACTICES PER 1 ACRE	SRI PRACTICES PER 1 ACRE
Nursery Management	30 to 40 kg seeds sowed on 0.1 acre flooded soils	3 to 5 kg seeds sowed on 0.01 acre mostly dry soils
Seedling Removal from Nursery	Removal of older, heavier seedlings usually at 30 days from flooded fields Time needed: 20 to 30 hours	Removal of younger, lighter seedlings at 8 to 20 days from muddy soil Time needed: 4 to 10 hours
Seedling Transport	WEIGHT CARRIED AT ONE TIME: 7 to 30 kg TOTAL WEIGHT TRANSPORTED: 400 to 1,200 kg TIME TO TRANSPORT SEEDLINGS: 5 to 30 hours WALKING DISTANCE: Nurseries are generally away from the main fields. Thus, more trips are needed to carry more seedlings to fields.	WEIGHT CARRIED AT ONE TIME: 5 to 6 kg TOTAL WEIGHT TRANSPORTED: 80 to 145 kg; up to 200 to 250 kg if seedlings are somewhat older. TIME TO TRANSPORT SEEDLINGS: 3 to 15 hours WALKING DISTANCE: As nurseries are often raised inside or near the main field, women make fewer trips and walk shorter distances.
Transplanting	TIME NEEDED: 90 to 160 hours Clumps of 4 to 6 seedlings are planted into flooded fields at random spacing.	TIME NEEDED: 70 to 120 hours Single seedlings are inserted carefully at wide spacing in rows into muddy soils.
Weeding	TIME NEEDED: 45 to 160 hours; repetitive standing and bending.	TIME NEEDED: 16 to 25 hours; upright posture with push weeder.
Harvesting	TIME NEEDED: 50 to 120 hours with simple scythe If the plants fall over due to weak stalks and are lying on the ground, they are harder to harvest, and the grains rot.	TIME NEEDED: 50 to 120 hours with simple scythe Plants and panicles are more uniform and thus easier to harvest but yields can be two to three times higher.

OPPOSITE: The many fewer and smaller seedlings women have to carry and handle under SRI **(TOP LEFT)** compared to conventional production **(TOP RIGHT)** dramatically reduces their workload.

BOTTOM LEFT: Despite billions of dollars invested in rice research by governments and the private sector, women still harvest rice with a simple scythe as they have for centuries.

BOTTOM RIGHT: With the introduction of the push-weeder women can weed fields in an upright position rather than bent over, and they can do the work faster. The weeder also aerates the soil, which contributes to higher yields.

JASMINE RICE AND HERB SALAD

SERVES 4

This simple salad is inspired by nasi ulam, a Malaysian rice salad made with plenty of herbs. Think of it as something to make when you have a large bunch of herbs in the refrigerator or a prolific herb garden. When choosing herbs to use, stick with the more tender-leaved ones, but don't be afraid to play around with the variety.

We kept the ingredient list pared back here, but you can experiment with adding other ingredients, like toasted dried shrimp powder (made by toasting dried shrimp in a skillet and pounding in a mortar), fried shallots, or slices of fresh chile.

1 small shallot, halved lengthwise and thinly sliced

Zest of 1 lime plus 1 Tbsp fresh lime juice, plus more as needed

Salt

Freshly ground pepper

3 Tbsp finely shredded unsweetened coconut

1 lemongrass stalk

1 cup [200 g] white jasmine rice, rinsed well, cooked (see page 48), and kept warm

1 packed cup [25 g] herbs, such as cilantro, Thai basil, rau răm, shiso, and/or mint, finely chopped

In a large bowl, combine the shallot with the lime zest and lime juice, season with salt and pepper, and let stand for at least 5 minutes.

In a small skillet over medium heat, toast the coconut until starting to brown, 1 to 2 minutes. Turn off the heat and stir, allowing the coconut to brown a bit more.

Chop off the top 4 in [10 cm] and the bottom of the lemongrass. Remove the tough outer pieces and save them to make tea or stock, if desired. Finely chop the tender inner core.

Add the rice and lemongrass to the bowl, season with salt and a little more lime juice, and toss. The rice should taste seasoned but not aggressively salty or acidic. Let cool slightly or fully to room temperature. When you're ready to serve, finely chop the herbs, add them to the salad, and toss again, then season with more salt and lime juice, if desired. Transfer to a bowl, sprinkle with the coconut, and serve.

CAULIFLOWER AND RED RICE SALAD
WITH PISTACHIOS AND HERBS

SERVES 4

Medium-grain red rice, like the one we import, has a hearty texture that's just wonderful in salads, especially in the fall. For this satisfying dish, which you could serve as a light main course or as a side, we roast cauliflower with baharat, an all-purpose Middle Eastern spice blend. (The one from artisanal food company NY Shuk is especially good.) If you can't find it, you can approximate it with a few common pantry spices. We then balance those warm notes with lots of flavorful herbs, sweet quick-pickled raisins, and crunchy pistachios.

Rice salads can handle a lot of seasoning, so don't be afraid to add more salt and lemon juice to help perk up the flavors, especially after it sits for a bit. We like to use parchment paper when roasting vegetables for ease of cleanup, but the cauliflower does become more richly browned when you roast without it.

1 medium head cauliflower, cored and cut into medium florets

5 Tbsp [80 ml] extra-virgin olive oil

2 tsp baharat or ½ tsp each ground cumin, coriander, cinnamon, and sweet paprika with a few turns of black pepper

Salt

1 lemon

1 small shallot, finely chopped

⅓ cup [45 g] raisins

2 Tbsp sherry vinegar

1 Tbsp warm water

1 cup [200 g] red rice, cooked and kept warm (see page 48)

⅓ cup [40 g] shelled pistachios, roughly chopped

Freshly ground pepper

½ cup [20 g] mixed tender herbs, such as dill, mint, cilantro, or tarragon

CONT'D

Set an oven rack in the lowest position and preheat the oven to 425°F [220°C]. Line a large baking sheet with parchment paper, if desired, for easier cleanup.

In a large bowl, toss the cauliflower with 3 Tbsp of the olive oil and the baharat. Season generously with salt and transfer to the prepared baking sheet.

Roast the cauliflower for 25 minutes, until browned on the bottom. Stir and roast until tender, 5 to 10 minutes longer. Finely grate the lemon zest over the cauliflower and squeeze the juice from half the lemon over the top, then toss.

Meanwhile, in a small bowl, combine the shallot, raisins, sherry vinegar, and water and let stand, tossing a few times, until the raisins are somewhat plump, about 20 minutes.

In the large bowl used for the cauliflower, combine the warm rice, cauliflower, raisin mixture, pistachios, and remaining 2 Tbsp of olive oil and toss together. Taste and season with salt and pepper and add more lemon juice from the remaining lemon half, if desired. Add the herbs and toss again, then serve warm or at room temperature.

MAKE AHEAD The rice salad can be refrigerated overnight. Bring to room temperature and re-season before serving.

SICILIAN-INSPIRED RICE SALAD

SERVES 4

This is the salad to make in the depths of winter when you're craving some sunshine and wish you could be whisked away to the shores of the Mediterranean. Rice, like potatoes and other grains, absorbs a lot of seasoning. When you first add the lemon juice, it might seem like too much, but the flavor mellows as it sits. You will also want to season the rice with salt twice—once while it's warm and a second time just before serving.

1 cup [200 g] Forbidden Rice® or other non-sticky black rice, cooked and kept warm (see page 48)

2 Tbsp fresh lemon juice

2 Tbsp extra-virgin olive oil

Salt

1 orange

½ cup [70 g] pitted green olives, such as Castelvetrano, thinly sliced

1 small fennel bulb, top removed, bulb quartered, cored, and thinly sliced

½ cup [6 g] parsley leaves, finely chopped

In a bowl, toss the warm rice with the lemon juice and olive oil and season with salt. Let cool to room temperature.

Using a Microplane grater, finely zest the orange over the rice. Using a sharp knife, remove the peel and bitter white pith from the orange. Slice the orange into rounds, then quarter the rounds and set them aside. Transfer any orange juice from cutting up the orange to the bowl.

Add the olives, fennel, and parsley to the rice and toss. Taste and season with more salt, if desired. Gently stir in the oranges and serve.

SESAME-GINGER NOODLE SALAD
WITH GREEN BEANS

**SERVES
4**

Cold sesame noodles are always a treat in summer, and really any time of year. This is a great dish to take along to a picnic or potluck. While you can prepare the salad a few hours ahead, try not to wait longer than that; it really tastes best the day it's made.

We use our organic brown rice udon noodles from Lotus Foods in this salad, which cook a bit differently than wheat-based udon. If you're using wheat udon, be sure to check the package instructions for guidance when cooking.

¼ cup [55 g] tahini

¼ cup [60 ml] soy sauce

2 Tbsp unseasoned rice vinegar

Juice of ½ lemon

2 tsp honey

1 tsp finely grated fresh ginger (from 1 in [2.5 cm] peeled ginger)

½ tsp chili-garlic sauce or sambal ulek, plus more for serving

1 lb [455 g] rice udon noodles

8 oz [230 g] green beans, cut into 1 in [2.5 cm] pieces

3 radishes, thinly sliced

Sliced green onions and toasted sesame seeds, for garnish

Bring a large soup pot of generously salted water to a boil.

Meanwhile, in a large bowl, whisk together the tahini, soy sauce, rice vinegar, lemon juice, honey, ginger, and chili-garlic sauce. Set aside.

Add the noodles to the water and cook until just tender, about 10 minutes. Using tongs, transfer the noodles to a strainer. Add the green beans to the water and cook until just tender, 1 to 3 minutes. Drain the noodles and green beans well, run under cold running water to cool, then shake out any excess water.

Add the noodles and green beans to the dressing and toss. Add the radishes and toss again, then garnish with green onions and sesame seeds. Serve with more chili-garlic sauce, if desired.

SUMMER RICE SALAD WITH TOMATOES, CORN, AND ROASTED PEPPERS

SERVES 4 TO 6

This is a salad to make after a walk through the farmers' market in August, when the tables overflow with a chromatic display of vegetables. It's a great light summer meal or dish to bring to a picnic. To add an intriguing depth of flavor, we quickly infuse olive oil with garlic before cooking the rice. We also blister the corn and roast the peppers on a grill or under a broiler, but if you prefer, you can include both of those ingredients raw. A single tablespoon of mayonnaise might seem so small that it's worth leaving out, but it really works to bring all the flavors together. Use vegan mayo if you prefer.

A sprinkle of feta cheese over this salad is a nice addition, but the finished dish is also delicious without it.

3 Tbsp extra-virgin olive oil, plus more for grilling

1 garlic clove, smashed

1 cup [200 g] brown jasmine rice or other short- or medium-grain brown rice, rinsed

Salt and freshly ground pepper

4 oz [115 g] green beans, trimmed and halved crosswise

Juice of 1 lime (about 3 Tbsp)

1 large shallot, thinly sliced

Pinch of sugar

4 medium ears of corn, husked

2 medium sweet red peppers, such as Jimmy Nardello or Italian frying peppers, or 1 red bell pepper

1 pt [320 g] Sungold or other cherry tomatoes, halved

1 Tbsp mayonnaise

1 cup [20 g] chopped cilantro or other tender herbs, such as mint or basil

CONT'D

In a medium saucepan over medium heat, warm 2 Tbsp of the olive oil. Add the garlic and cook, tipping the pan so the oil pools, until the garlic is softened and fragrant. Remove the garlic clove and reserve for another use. Add the rice and stir to coat with the oil, then add 1¾ cup [420 ml] of water and season with salt and pepper. Bring to a boil over high heat, cover, and lower the heat to medium-low. Simmer the rice until the water is absorbed and the rice is tender, 30 to 40 minutes. Turn off the heat, add the green beans to the pot, then re-cover and let stand for 5 minutes. Uncover and use a wooden spoon to fluff the rice.

Meanwhile, in a large bowl, combine the lime juice, shallot, a pinch of salt, and a pinch of sugar and toss to combine. Let stand as you prepare the rest of the salad.

Preheat a grill or a broiler to high heat. Rub the corn and peppers lightly with oil. Grill the corn and peppers, turning occasionally, until the corn is blistered in spots and the pepper skin is completely blackened, about 10 minutes. Alternatively, set the corn and peppers on a baking sheet and broil about 4 in [10 cm] from the heat, turning once halfway through, until the corn is blistered in spots and the pepper skin is blackened, about 10 minutes total. (You might need to adjust the position of the vegetables under the broiler so they cook evenly.)

Transfer the corn to a work surface and the peppers to a bowl. Cover the peppers with another bowl so the pepper skin loosens. When the corn is cool enough to handle, use a serrated knife to remove the kernels, cutting down the cobs. Add the kernels to the large bowl with the shallot mixture and season with salt and pepper. Rub off and discard the skins from the peppers, remove the stem and seeds, and cut the pepper flesh into strips. Transfer the peppers to the bowl and season with salt and pepper.

Add the rice, green beans, tomatoes, mayonnaise, and remaining 1 Tbsp of olive oil. Season with salt and pepper and toss to combine. Let stand for 10 minutes to let the flavors meld, then add the herbs to the salad, and toss.

Taste the salad once more and season with more salt or lime juice, if necessary, then serve at room temperature.

OKRA RICE

SERVES 4

Okra, an African vegetable, is also beloved in American Southern, Caribbean, and Indian cooking. You often find okra paired with rice in dishes from the Gullah Geechee—the descendants of enslaved Africans who traditionally lived in the coastal areas and the sea islands of North Carolina, South Carolina, Georgia, and Florida—as well as in Trinidad and Jamaica. This version is inspired by okra dishes from Trinidad, where you might also find salt cod in them. The beauty of cooking okra and rice together is that the rice absorbs okra's natural moisture, and the okra turns silky in the pot. You can use fresh or frozen okra in this dish.

2 Tbsp extra-virgin olive oil

1 medium yellow onion, chopped

2 garlic cloves, thinly sliced

Salt and freshly ground pepper

1 tsp finely grated fresh ginger (from 1 in [2.5 cm] peeled ginger)

¼ cup [10 g] finely chopped cilantro, plus more for serving

12 oz [340 g] okra, trimmed and cut crosswise into ½ in [13 mm] pieces, or one 8 oz [230 g] bag of frozen okra cuts

1 Tbsp tomato paste

1½ cups [360 ml] vegetable broth

½ Scotch bonnet or habanero chile

1 cup [200 g] basmati or other long-grain white rice, rinsed (see page 41)

In a large, heavy pot over medium heat, warm the olive oil. Add the onion and garlic, season with salt and pepper, and cook, stirring, until translucent, about 8 minutes. Add the ginger and cilantro and cook until fragrant and no longer raw smelling, about 30 seconds. Add the okra, season with salt, and cook, stirring, until bright green, 2 minutes. Add the tomato paste and cook, stirring, until it starts to glaze the bottom of the pan, 2 minutes.

Add the broth and chile, bring to a simmer, and cook, scraping up any browned bits from the bottom of the pan, 1 minute. Add the rice and season with salt and stir to incorporate, then lower the heat to low. Cover and cook until the rice is tender and the liquid is absorbed, 20 minutes.

Turn off the heat and let stand for 5 minutes. Fluff the rice, remove the chile, and taste. Season with more salt and pepper, if desired. Sprinkle with more cilantro and serve.

MISO-GLAZED EGGPLANT WITH SEAWEED RICE

SERVES 4

This dish reminds us of something you might find at the salad bar in a health food store, but in the best way. It's gently sweet and umami rich. Arame seaweed lends a delicate flavor while hijiki is more prominent. You can usually find one or the other at a health food store.

FOR THE SEAWEED RICE

½ cup [7 g] arame or hijiki seaweed

1 Tbsp soy sauce

1½ tsp unseasoned rice vinegar

1½ tsp honey

½ tsp toasted sesame oil

1 cup [200 g] brown rice (any type), cooked and kept warm (see page 48)

Salt

FOR THE EGGPLANT

1 lb [455 g] eggplant, cut into ¾ in [2 cm] pieces

3 Tbsp canola oil

Salt

2 Tbsp white miso

½ tsp grated fresh ginger (from ½ in [13 mm] peeled ginger)

2 tsp honey

1½ tsp unseasoned rice vinegar

1 tsp toasted sesame oil

Sliced green onions, for serving

TO MAKE THE SEAWEED RICE, in a bowl, cover the seaweed with cool water and let stand until tender, 15 to 20 minutes. Drain and pat dry.

In a large bowl, combine the soy sauce, rice vinegar, honey, and sesame oil. Add the seaweed and let stand for 5 minutes. Add the rice and gently stir together. Season with salt.

MEANWHILE, TO PREPARE THE EGGPLANT, preheat the oven to 350°F [180°C] and line a baking sheet with parchment paper. On the baking sheet, toss the eggplant with the canola oil, season lightly with salt, and spread it out into an even layer. Roast the eggplant until just starting to turn tender, about 15 minutes. Let cool slightly. Increase the oven temperature to 450°F [230°C].

In a bowl, whisk together the miso, 1 Tbsp of water, the ginger, honey, rice vinegar, and sesame oil. Transfer the eggplant to the bowl with the miso glaze, and toss. Return the eggplant to the baking sheet.

Roast the eggplant, stirring halfway through, until browned, 15 minutes. Let cool slightly, then transfer to the rice and toss. Season with salt, then serve with green onions.

RICE AND BLACK BEANS WITH COCONUT MILK AND THYME

SERVES 4 TO 6

Rice and legumes is a comfort food staple throughout much of the rice-eating world, with versions varying from country to country and even from cook to cook. Some cooks from Latin America make a yellow rice tinged with turmeric or tomato or annatto seeds. Some people use pigeon peas or field peas (like black-eyed peas) while others reach for common bean varieties including red beans, pinto beans, and black beans. The seasonings vary widely and can be fiery hot or quite mild.

This version is inspired by the way some cooks in the Caribbean use coconut milk and thyme in their rice and beans. If you'd like to make a spicy version, add a whole or half Scotch bonnet or habanero chile to the liquid, then remove it at the end of the cook time.

One 13½ oz [385 ml] can coconut milk

2 Tbsp extra-virgin olive oil

1 large yellow onion, finely chopped

2 garlic cloves, thinly sliced

Salt and freshly ground pepper

1 tsp fresh thyme leaves, or ½ tsp dried thyme

1½ cups [300 g] basmati or other long-grain white rice, rinsed (see page 41)

One 15 oz [430 g] can black beans, drained and rinsed

In a large measuring cup, measure out the coconut milk, then add enough water to equal 2¼ cups [540 ml] of liquid. Set aside.

In a saucepan with a tight-fitting lid over medium heat, warm the olive oil. Add the onion and garlic, season generously with salt and pepper, and cook, stirring, until softened, about 5 minutes. Add the thyme and cook until fragrant, about 2 minutes.

Add the rice, beans, and coconut milk mixture and season with salt. Bring to a boil over medium-high heat, then lower the heat to medium-low, cover, and cook until tender, 20 to 25 minutes. Turn off the heat and let stand for 5 minutes. Uncover and fluff the rice and beans, seasoning with more salt, if desired. Serve warm.

BLACK RICE MUJADARA

SERVES 4

Mujadara, a popular Middle Eastern combination of rice and lentils, is one of those dishes that shows off the magic of beautifully browned onions. When combined with a little cumin, you have all you need to turn some humble staples into a dish worth craving.

1 cup [200 g] Forbidden Rice® or other non-sticky black rice

Salt

1 cup [200 g] French green lentils

¼ cup [60 ml] extra-virgin olive oil

5 medium yellow onions, halved and thinly sliced

1 tsp ground cumin

Chopped parsley, sliced radishes, and plain whole-milk yogurt (optional), for serving

In a large pot, combine the rice with 2 qt [2 L] of water and season generously with salt; bring to a boil over high heat. When the water boils, lower the heat to medium, add the lentils, and simmer until the rice and lentils are tender, 20 to 25 minutes. Drain, then return to the pot. Taste and season with salt.

Meanwhile, in a large skillet over medium heat, warm the oil. Add the onions, season generously with salt, and cook, stirring until the onions are translucent, 8 minutes. Increase the heat to medium-high and cook, stirring occasionally, until the onions are browned and browned bits are sticking to the skillet, 15 minutes. Add 1 Tbsp of water and cook, stirring and scraping up the browned bits, until the water has evaporated and the onions start to stick again. Add 1 more Tbsp of water and cook, stirring, until the onions are nicely golden and very soft, 2 minutes. Add the cumin and cook, stirring, until fragrant, 1 minute.

Scoop out one-quarter of the onions. Add the rice and lentils to the onions in the pan and stir until hot. Transfer to a platter and top with the reserved onions. Garnish with parsley and radishes and serve with yogurt, if desired.

CARROT RICE WITH PISTACHIOS AND DRIED APRICOTS

SERVES 4

This sweet and savory rice dish is inspired by the types you might find on a Persian table, often served with chicken. While saffron is optional here, do use it if you can. It tints the rice with a warm, golden hue and makes it taste especially lovely.

¼ cup [45 g] dried apricots, thinly sliced

1 small pinch saffron (about 4 threads, optional)

2 Tbsp extra-virgin olive oil

1 medium yellow onion, chopped

Salt

2 garlic cloves, thinly sliced

4 oz [115 g] carrots, shredded with a food processor or grated by hand

½ tsp caraway seeds or cumin seeds

½ tsp ground ginger

1 cup [200 g] white or brown basmati rice, cooked (see page 48)

1 Tbsp honey

¼ cup [30 g] shelled roasted and salted pistachios, roughly chopped

Chopped parsley, for serving

Bring a small saucepan of water to a boil.

Place the apricots in a small bowl and pour in enough boiling water just to cover. Let stand until plump.

In another small bowl, combine the saffron, if using, and 1 Tbsp of the boiling water.

In a large skillet over medium heat, warm the olive oil. Add the onion, season with salt, and cook until starting to soften, 5 minutes. Add the garlic and cook until softened, 2 minutes.

Add the carrots, season with salt, and cook until starting to soften, 1 to 2 minutes. Add the caraway and ginger and cook until fragrant, 30 seconds.

Add the rice to the skillet and cook, stirring, until incorporated. Add the saffron threads and their liquid and the honey and cook, stirring, until incorporated. Turn off the heat.

Drain the apricots and add to the rice along with the pistachios and toss. Season the rice with salt, sprinkle with parsley, and serve.

BASMATI AND PEA PULAO

SERVES 8

We source heirloom Dehraduni basmati rice from organic farmer families in northern India who practice regenerative agriculture. The grains are long and elegant and almost impossibly slender. This dish comes from Laxmi Devi Saxena, one of the rice farmers we work with in Budaun in the state of Uttar Pradesh, which sits on the border with Nepal.

Cooked with ghee (golden clarified butter you can purchase in jars at many supermarkets) and spices, the rice becomes wonderfully fluffy, like a fragrant pile of confetti. This recipe calls for whole spices, which bring more nuanced flavors to the dish. When serving, you can pull them out or remind guests to push them to the side. If you're serving a smaller group, you can easily halve this recipe, but it's worth making the whole batch because it tastes delicious reheated the next day.

One 1 in [2.5 cm] piece ginger, peeled and cut into coins	8 whole cloves	2 jalapeños, quartered lengthwise, seeded if desired, and finely chopped	½ cup [70 g] roasted salted cashews, lightly crushed	Whole-milk yogurt, for serving (optional)
2 garlic cloves, smashed	5 green cardamom pods, left whole	Leaves from 4 mint sprigs, finely chopped	2 cups [400 g] white Dehraduni basmati rice or other basmati, soaked for 20 minutes, then drained well (see page 41)	
4 Tbsp [55 g] ghee	½ tsp cumin seeds			
2 bay leaves	2 medium yellow onions, thinly sliced	4 cilantro sprigs, finely chopped		
2 cinnamon sticks	Salt and freshly ground pepper	1 cup [120 g] frozen peas		

In a mortar or mini food processor, pound or pulse the ginger and garlic to a paste.

In a large, heavy soup pot with a tight-fitting lid over medium heat, melt 2 Tbsp of the ghee. Add the bay leaves, cinnamon sticks, cloves, cardamom, and cumin seeds and cook, stirring, just until they begin to sizzle, about 30 seconds. Add the onions, season generously with salt and pepper, and cook, stirring, until starting to turn golden, about 10 minutes. Add the jalapeños and cook until fragrant, about 2 minutes. Add the garlic and ginger and cook, stirring constantly, until they seem to melt into the onions, 1 to 2 minutes. Add the mint, cilantro, peas, and cashews, season with salt and pepper, and cook until fragrant, about 2 minutes.

Add 2½ cups [600 ml] of water and bring to a boil over high heat. Add the drained rice and season with salt. Lower the heat to medium-low, cover the pot, and cook until the rice is tender and the liquid is fully absorbed, about 20 minutes. Remove from the heat and let stand for 5 minutes. Stir in the remaining 2 Tbsp of ghee. Taste and season with more salt, if desired, then serve as a side dish or with yogurt for a light meal.

JOLLOF RICE

**SERVES
6 TO 8**

Jollof rice, a well-known West African dish, is thought to have
influenced many rice dishes in the American South, like red rice and
Creole-style jambalaya. Like so many classic rice dishes, jollof rice
varies from region to region and cook to cook, and cooks love to
debate everything from the seasoning to the type of rice used to the
cooking method. No matter the argument, cooks agree that the dish
should always be incredibly flavorful.

It's often made by first creating a spicy tomato-pepper sauce,
which can be prepared a day in advance. The rice is then cooked with
that sauce along with many other seasonings and a flavorful broth
(which is sometimes made with bouillon cubes or Maggi seasoning)
until the grains are fluffy and separate. Sometimes, meat or fish are
cooked right in the jollof rice. Other times, they're served alongside.

To prevent any scorching, we use the method writer and recipe
developer Yewande Komolafe uses for her recipe in the *New York
Times*, and cook the rice in the oven. Some people prefer their jollof
rice to have a smoky flavor, which can come from allowing the rice
to brown or even slightly scorch on the bottom. To achieve that, set
your uncovered pot of cooked jollof rice over medium heat and cook,
monitoring the bottom of the pot, until the rice starts to brown on
the bottom.

Jollof rice is often a party food, so it's best prepared in a big
batch. (This one is relatively small compared to other recipes.) It's
one rice dish that holds up beautifully at room temperature and
makes for delicious leftovers. If you have any chicken drippings, you
will not regret adding them to the rice after cooking.

To help the basmati rice we use here cook evenly, it's best to soak
it first.

FOR THE TOMATO-PEPPER SAUCE				
1 lb [455 g] plum tomatoes, cored and chopped	½ large red onion, roughly chopped Cloves from ½ head of garlic, peeled	1 large red bell pepper, cored, seeded, and roughly chopped	1 to 2 Scotch bonnet or habanero chiles, stemmed but not seeded	¼ cup [60 ml] canola oil Salt **CONT'D**

TO MAKE THE TOMATO-PEPPER SAUCE, in a blender, purée the tomatoes, onion, garlic, bell pepper, and chile.

In a wide saucepan over medium heat, warm the oil. Add the purée, stir, bring to a simmer, and cook until it's thick enough that it starts to spatter, about 10 minutes. Lower the heat to medium-low and continue cooking until the sauce is reduced to 1½ cups [360 ml], about 20 minutes longer. Let the sauce cool to warm and season with salt.

TO MAKE THE JOLLOF RICE, preheat the oven to 350°F [180°C].

In a large, heavy ovenproof soup pot or Dutch oven with a tight-fitting lid over medium heat, warm the oil. Add the onion, season generously with salt, and cook, stirring, until softened, 6 to 8 minutes. Add the onion powder, curry powder, garlic powder, and thyme and cook, stirring, until fragrant, about 20 seconds. Add the rice, stir to coat with the seasonings, then add the tomato-pepper sauce and broth.

Increase the heat to high and bring to a simmer, then remove from the heat and cover. Transfer the pot with the rice to the oven and cook for 20 minutes, or until all the liquid is absorbed and the rice is tender. (A very thin layer of reduced tomato-pepper sauce will rise to the top, and that's okay.) Remove the pot from the oven and let stand for 5 minutes. Fluff the rice, stirring to incorporate the sauce, season with more salt, if desired, and serve.

FOR THE JOLLOF RICE

3 Tbsp canola oil

½ large red onion, thinly sliced

Salt

1 Tbsp onion powder

1 tsp curry powder, such as Jamaican curry or madras

1 tsp garlic powder

1 tsp dried thyme or 1 Tbsp fresh thyme leaves

2 cups white basmati rice, rinsed well, soaked for 30 minutes, then drained well (see page 41)

2½ cups [600 ml] low-sodium chicken or vegetable broth, or water

STICKY RICE WITH MUSHROOMS

SERVES
4 TO 6

While sticky rice pops up frequently in desserts in Asia, it's also deeply satisfying when paired with savory flavors. Sticky rice doesn't appear in every supermarket, but you can find it online and at most Asian markets. To cook it so it's sticky and chewy but not mushy, it's important to soak it in advance and then steam it, so be sure to plan ahead.

We make this dish using French-style duxelles, which are finely chopped mushrooms cooked down so they almost form a spread. Instead of the usual shallot and thyme mixture, we season the duxelles with ginger and garlic as well as Chinese Shaoxing and soy sauce.

You can use any type of mushrooms to make this dish, but we're especially fond of a mix that includes maitake, also known as hen of the woods, as well as button mushrooms.

1½ cups [300 g] white sticky rice

1 lb [455 g] mixed mushrooms, cleaned and trimmed so any tough stems are removed

2 garlic cloves, finely grated

2 tsp finely grated fresh ginger (from 2 in [5 cm] peeled ginger)

3 Tbsp soy sauce, plus more as needed

2 tsp sugar

2 Tbsp canola oil

Salt and freshly ground white pepper

¼ cup [60 ml] Shaoxing or dry sherry or dry white wine (see Note)

Thinly sliced chive or green onions, for serving

In a strainer, rinse the rice well and drain. Transfer to a bowl, cover with water, and soak for 4 to 12 hours, then drain again.

Line a steamer basket or fine-mesh sieve with cheesecloth so it overhangs the edge and transfer the rice to it. Fill a soup pot that holds the steamer basket or sieve with about 1 in [2.5 cm] of water. Set the rice in the steamer basket over the water, cover, and bring to a boil. When the water boils, steam the rice for 15 minutes. Remove the rice from the steamer basket and use the overhang of the cheesecloth to carefully flip the solid disk of sticky rice onto a plate. Return the cheesecloth to the basket and the rice to the cheesecloth so the cooked

CONT'D

Shaoxing wine is a Chinese wine made from fermenting brown rice and a small amount of wheat. It's amber in color and has a complex flavor. You can often find it online, in East Asian markets and some grocery stores. If you can't find it, you can substitute dry sherry or, in this case, dry white wine. While neither will have the same flavor as Shaoxing, it will still be delicious.

side is now up, then return to the pot. Steam the rice until cooked through but not mushy, about 15 minutes longer. Remove the rice from the heat but keep covered until ready to use.

Meanwhile, in a food processor, pulse the mushrooms, garlic, and ginger until finely chopped, 20 to 30 pulses.

In a small bowl, stir together 2 Tbsp of the soy sauce with the sugar. Set aside.

In a large, deep skillet over medium-high heat, warm the oil until shimmering. Add the mushroom mixture, season with salt and pepper, and cook, stirring frequently, until the mushrooms release their liquid and then the liquid evaporates and the mushrooms start to brown, about 10 minutes. Add the Shaoxing and cook, stirring, until the liquid evaporates, about 3 minutes. Add the soy sauce mixture and cook, stirring, until just incorporated.

Add the sticky rice to the mushrooms and cook, stirring, until the mushrooms and sticky rice are incorporated. Add the remaining 1 Tbsp of soy sauce and stir until the rice is moistened. Season with more salt, pepper, and soy sauce, if desired. Garnish with chives or green onions and serve hot.

LEMONY RICE WITH SPINACH AND DILL

SERVES 4

This rice pilaf takes its flavor cues from Greece. We like to use our Lotus Foods tricolor rice, which includes red and brown rice varieties from Indonesia, but any medium-grain brown rice works well. Serve alongside fish or chicken, or of course you can put an egg on it!

One 5 oz [140 g] bag baby spinach

2 Tbsp extra-virgin olive oil

½ medium yellow onion, chopped

2 garlic cloves, thinly sliced

Salt and freshly ground pepper

1 cup [200 g] Tricolor Blend Rice or medium-grain brown rice

1¾ cup [420 ml] low-sodium chicken or vegetable broth

Zest of 1 lemon plus juice from ½ lemon, plus more as needed

¼ cup [10 g] chopped dill

In a heavy medium saucepan with a tight-fitting lid over medium heat, combine ¼ cup [60 ml] of water with the spinach and cook, stirring occasionally, until wilted and most of the water has evaporated, 1 to 2 minutes. Transfer the spinach to a cutting board and let cool slightly, then coarsely chop.

In the same saucepan, heat the olive oil over medium heat. Add the onion and garlic, season with salt and pepper, and cook until softened, about 6 minutes. Add the rice and broth and stir once, then bring to a boil. Lower the heat to medium-low, season with more salt and pepper, cover, and simmer until the rice is tender and the liquid is absorbed, 30 to 40 minutes.

Remove from the heat and let stand for 5 minutes. Add the lemon zest and juice followed by the spinach and dill and stir to combine. Taste and season with enough salt so there is a pleasant tension between the flavors of the lemon and salt. Serve warm.

MAKE AHEAD The rice can be refrigerated overnight. Reheat gently.

SWISS CHARD STUFFED WITH BLACK RICE, ALMONDS, AND CURRANTS

SERVES 4

Silky Swiss chard stuffed with a flavorful filling is a delicious side dish to all kinds of meals and can also become a satisfying vegetarian main course. Sweet currants add an unexpected pop of sweetness that's just right with the tomato sauce.

FOR THE SIMPLE TOMATO SAUCE (OR USE 2 CUPS [480 ML] OF YOUR FAVORITE TOMATO SAUCE)

¼ cup [60 ml] extra-virgin olive oil

1 small yellow onion, finely chopped

2 garlic cloves, thinly sliced

Pinch of red pepper flakes

Salt

2 cups [480 ml] tomato passata (uncooked tomato purée)

FOR THE FILLING

½ cup [50 g] sliced almonds

3 Tbsp extra-virgin olive oil

1 small yellow onion, chopped

3 garlic cloves, thinly sliced

12 large Swiss chard leaves (plus a few extra in case of ripping), thick ribs and stems removed and chopped, leaves kept whole

Salt

1 cup [200 g] Forbidden Rice® or other non-sticky black rice

½ cup [70 g] dried currants

TO MAKE THE TOMATO SAUCE, in a saucepan over medium heat, warm the olive oil. Add the onion, garlic, and red pepper flakes, season with salt, and cook, stirring occasionally, until the onions are very soft, about 8 minutes. Add the tomato passata and bring to a boil over medium-high heat. Lower the heat to medium-low and simmer, stirring occasionally, until slightly thickened and very flavorful, 20 to 30 minutes. Season with more salt, as desired.

TO MAKE THE FILLING, in a small skillet over medium heat, toast the almonds, stirring frequently, until fragrant, 2 to 3 minutes. Transfer to a plate.

In a medium soup pot with a tight-fitting lid over medium heat, warm the olive oil. Add the onion, garlic, and sliced Swiss chard stems. Season generously with salt and cook, stirring occasionally, until the onions are softened, about 8 minutes. Add the rice, 1¾ cups [420 ml] of water, and the currants and bring to a boil over high heat.

CONT'D

Lower the heat to medium-low, cover, and cook until the rice is tender, 30 to 35 minutes. Remove from the heat and let the rice stand, covered, for 5 minutes, then let the filling cool to warm before using.

Meanwhile, bring a large pot of salted water to a boil. Add the Swiss chard leaves a few at a time and cook until bright green and pliable, about 10 seconds. Using tongs, transfer them to a work surface or plate and let cool.

Preheat the oven to 375°F [190°C].

Working with one leaf at a time, arrange about ¼ cup [65 g] of the rice filling in the center of the leaf. Fold the stem end over the filling and then tuck in the sides. Roll the leaf over to form a bundle, overlapping the ends to seal. Transfer, seam-side down, to a 9 by 9 in [23 by 23 cm] or similar-sized baking dish. Repeat with the remaining leaves and filling.

Pour the tomato sauce over the stuffed chard and cover the pan with parchment paper followed by aluminum foil.

Bake for about 30 minutes, until the sauce is bubbling and the leaves are very tender. Serve hot or warm.

MAKE AHEAD The assembled stuffed chard can be refrigerated overnight. Bake as directed.

LIMITING OUR EXPOSURE
TO ARSENIC IN RICE

Arsenic is an element in the environment that is found naturally in rocks and soil, water, air, and plants and animals. It can also be released into the environment from mining pollution, other industrial sources, and prior agricultural practices that utilized arsenic pesticide. We normally take in small amounts of arsenic in the air we breathe, the water we drink, and the food we eat. Arsenic is found in many food products, including rice, seafood, poultry, juices, coffee, beer, cheese, vegetables, mushrooms, bread, and chocolate.

In recent years, rice has been in the news because it can contain elevated amounts of arsenic, both organic and inorganic. When humans are overexposed to inorganic arsenic, it increases their risk for some cancers. What elevates arsenic in rice is that it is generally grown submerged in water (anaerobic, or without oxygen), so if

arsenic is present in the soil or water, it can increase concentrations in the rice plant. Growing rice aerobically—so the fields are not continually flooded—can decrease the amount of arsenic in the rice. This is another reason why we like to support farmers who use the More Crop Per Drop™ method, also known as SRI (see page 55 for more).

Studies have shown that whole-grain rice varieties tend to retain more arsenic than milled white varieties when grown in similar conditions. Rinsing rice can decrease the amount of arsenic in rice, as can soaking and then discarding the water. Except for guidance on limits of inorganic arsenic in apple juice and rice in infant cereal, there is currently no general US standard for arsenic in rice or food. For more information about how to limit exposure to arsenic in food and dietary supplements, the US Food and Drug Administration website is a good resource.

4

MAIN DISHES

RICE IS CULTURE

Through the many countries we've traveled, whether China, Thailand, Indonesia, India, or Madagascar, rice is at the center of the table, nourishing families every day and during celebrations. It's held sacred by many and is filled with lore and superstition, sometimes inspiring fervent defense of one way of washing, cooking, or eating it.

In some East and Southeast Asian countries, rice is so important that the literal translation of the phrase used to ask, "How are you?" is "Have you eaten rice today?" According to culinary historian Michael Twitty's book *Rice*, in Sierra Leone, if you haven't eaten rice, some say you haven't eaten at all.

When you look at some of the great rice cultures of the world, you often see how rice dishes traversed continents, telling hopeful and horrible stories of migration. For instance, the earliest version of pilau—long-grain rice cooked with aromatics and silky fat to create flavorful and fluffy rice dishes—likely originated in Ancient Persia. With the spread of Islam and the trade route known as the Silk Road, similar dishes popped up in northern India and northern China, where you find pulao; in Turkey, where you have pilaf; and Spain, which is famous for its rice dish known as paella. When British colonists brought indentured servants from India to Trinidad, so came pelau, incorporating local ingredients as well as techniques from the African and Spanish cooks who lived there.

Rice began its journey to the "New World" in the mid-1500s with Spanish and Portuguese colonizers. Portuguese traders enslaved

Africans to work on sugar plantations being established in the colony of Brazil. They provisioned their ships with milled and unhusked seed rice from West Africa's coastal communities, as well as other African crops like okra, pigeon peas, black-eyed peas, millet, sorghum, yams, and African palm oil. During this same time period, traders took the seeds of tomatoes, peppers, and other "New World" crops to Europe and Africa, forever changing their cuisines—and their rice dishes.

As early as 1609, rice was promoted as a potential commodity for the American colonies, with some Virginia colonists growing it in the same way they did other dryland crops like barley. It wasn't until the end of the 1600s that rice production took off in South Carolina. Enslavers brought expert rice growers and processors from West Africa, especially women, and forced them to use their knowledge and labor to grow rice in the lowland swampy environments similar to their homelands. By 1700, enslaved people in South Carolina produced more rice for export than there were ships in port to carry it across the Atlantic, creating staggering wealth for landowners and generations of inequality. According to geographer Judith Carney, who has spent decades studying the topic, "A crucial component of the successful establishment of rice cultivation in South Carolina was the transfer of a farming and crop processing system deeply associated with female knowledge."

Even as commercial rice cultivation dwindled in the region after a series of storms at the end of the nineteenth century and beginning of the twentieth, the freed African descendants in the Carolina Lowcountry, known as the Gullah Geechee, kept their rice culture and rice cuisine alive for generations. With chefs like BJ Dennis and community activists like Sara Green (page 159, top right) working to preserve this cuisine and new books and articles devoted to it, the Gullah Geechee and their foodways are finally getting the spotlight they deserve.

It's undeniable that the preference for dry-style rice in the South and the origin of many Southern rice dishes—including those from the Lowcountry, like Hoppin' John, and the Creole dishes of the Gulf Coast, like gumbo—come directly from enslaved West African cooks. Some of these dishes use techniques similar to making pilau—so the rice is cooked with aromatic vegetables and sometimes meat in a wonderfully flavorful liquid. A number of Southern rice dishes, such as red rice and Spanish rice, include both tomatoes and peppers. And it's no surprise that in countries like Senegal and Ghana, where so many enslaved people were taken from and forced to come to the nascent United States and farm rice, you find similar dishes like jollof rice (page 145), which remain popular staples to this day.

After slavery was abolished in many European colonies and eventually in the United States, indentured laborers from China and other parts of Asia moved to these areas, bringing their own styles of rice, rice cookery, and rice culture, resulting in notable cultural exchanges and infinite varieties of fried rice. For example, in Jamaica, you might find fried rice seasoned with fiery hot Scotch bonnet peppers, while in Peru, cumin is a frequent addition and lime wedges are often served on the side. Migration and merging of rice cultures around the world continues to this day. For example, starting in the 1970s, thousands of Vietnamese refugees settled in coastal Louisiana, and the region is now known for its Viet-Cajun dishes.

It's tempting to try to seek out "authentic" versions of traditional rice dishes, but authenticity is subjective because food culture is always evolving. Most of the people who rely on rice for their daily sustenance grow their own rice or eat rice grown nearby. The varieties and cooking styles can vary immensely based on the climate, traditions, and even personal preferences, with some people enjoying drier rice while others favoring stickier rice. At the same time, exploitation of cultural foodways of Black, Latinx, and Asian people is real and should be discouraged. In the United States, we are incredibly privileged to have so many varieties at hand—from luxuriously fluffy Indian pulao to Chinese fried rice to Italian risotto to West African jollof rice. Regardless of who is doing the cooking, food with such a rich history should be treated with respect.

When we sit down to enjoy rice, we often think about the many people all over the world and throughout history who have relied on this life-sustaining grain and the farmers who have worked so hard to bring rice to us. We also think about the cooks who moved around the world, some seeking better lives and others not by choice, who took cooking techniques they knew from home and combined them with local ingredients to create something entirely new and beautiful. We hope you'll do the same.

KIMCHI FRIED RICE WITH SHIITAKE AND EDAMAME

SERVES 4

Kimchi—Korean salted and fermented vegetables (usually Napa cabbage)—can bring so much flavor to a dish. Here, cabbage kimchi is lightly caramelized, creating extra complexity in this fried rice. If you prefer a tangier-tasting kimchi and want to maintain its probiotics, skip the cooking step and add it to the fried rice just before serving.

One 1 lb [455 g] jar cabbage kimchi

¼ cup plus 2 Tbsp [90 ml] canola oil

8 oz [230g] shiitake mushrooms, stems removed, caps sliced

1 tsp grated fresh ginger (from 1 in [2.5 cm] peeled ginger)

3 Tbsp soy sauce

1 Tbsp sugar

1 cup [120 g] frozen shelled edamame

3 cups [360 g] cooked rice, day-old if white (see page 46)

1 tsp toasted sesame oil

Toasted sesame seeds, for garnish

Open your jar of kimchi and see how big the pieces are. If they seem too big to eat in one bite, use scissors to snip them into manageable pieces. Reserve any liquid.

In a large wok or well-seasoned cast-iron skillet over medium heat, heat ¼ cup [60 ml] of the oil. Add the mushrooms and cook, stirring, until softened, 4 minutes. Add the ginger, stir, and cook until fragrant, 1 minute. Add 2 Tbsp of the soy sauce and cook, stirring, until thickened slightly, 1 minute. Scrape the mushrooms into a bowl. Wipe out the wok.

In the same wok over medium-high heat, warm the remaining 2 Tbsp of oil. Add the kimchi with its liquid and the sugar and cook, stirring, until the kimchi juices are evaporated and the kimchi starts to blister in spots, 5 to 10 minutes, depending on the juiciness of the kimchi. Add the edamame and cook, tossing, until hot, 1 minute. Add the rice and stir, breaking up any clumps. Add the mushrooms, remaining 1 Tbsp of soy sauce, and sesame oil and cook, stirring, until everything is incorporated. Garnish with sesame seeds and serve.

BEET RICE BOWLS WITH AVOCADO-CHICKPEA SPREAD

SERVES 4

Inspired by ceviche—lime-marinated fish popular in coastal areas of Latin America—we toss cooked beets with lime juice, green onions, and chiles. Arame seaweed brings in a deeper flavor and a whisper of the sea.

Black rice looks especially gorgeous with the beets and the chickpea-avocado spread—a cross between hummus and guacamole. To help this dish come together faster, you can use the precooked vacuum-sealed beets you find in the grocery store.

FOR THE BEETS

1 lb [455 g] beets, without tops, scrubbed

2 Tbsp arame seaweed (optional)

Juice of 1 lime, plus more if desired

3 green onions, thinly sliced

½ jalapeño, seeded if desired and thinly sliced

Salt

FOR THE AVOCADO-CHICKPEA SPREAD

One 15 oz [430 g] can chickpeas with their liquid

1 ripe Hass avocado

¼ cup [35 g] toasted pumpkin seeds

1 small garlic clove

½ cup [6 g] cilantro leaves

½ jalapeño, seeded if desired and coarsely chopped

Juice of ½ lime, plus more if desired

2 Tbsp extra-virgin olive oil

Salt

FOR SERVING

1½ cups [300 g] Forbidden Rice® or other non-sticky black rice, cooked (see page 48)

Cilantro, for garnish

CONT'D

TO MAKE THE BEETS, fill a medium saucepan with 1 in [2.5 cm] of water and add a steamer basket if you have one. (If you don't, that's okay.) Add the beets to the basket or directly to the water and bring to a boil over high heat. Lower the heat to medium-low, cover, and cook until the beets are tender when pierced with a knife, 40 minutes to 1 hour, depending on the size of your beets.

Transfer the beets to a work surface and let cool. When they're cool enough to handle, remove the skins. (You might want to wear gloves since red beets will stain your hands.) The skins should rub right off, or use a peeler to gently remove.

Chop the cooked beets into bite-size pieces and transfer to a bowl.

Meanwhile, in a small bowl, cover the arame, if using, with cool water and let stand until softened, about 10 minutes. Drain, then squeeze dry. Add the arame to the beets.

Add the lime juice, green onions, and jalapeño to the beets, then season generously with salt. Let stand for 30 minutes, stirring occasionally, or refrigerate for up to 4 hours. Stir the beets and taste; add more lime juice and salt, if desired.

TO MAKE THE SPREAD, in a food processor or blender, combine the chickpeas with their liquid, avocado flesh, pumpkin seeds, garlic, cilantro, and jalapeño and pulse until finely chopped, 10 to 15 pulses. With the machine running, add the lime juice and olive oil and purée until smooth, adding a little water if needed if it's too thick. (A blender will make a smoother spread while a food processor will give more texture.) Taste the spread and season generously with salt, then add more lime juice, if desired.

TO SERVE, scoop some of the spread into bowls and arrange the beets on top. Set some black rice alongside, garnish the bowls with cilantro, then serve.

JADE RICE BOWLS WITH BROCCOLI, TOFU, AND AVOCADO "RANCH"

SERVES 4

For those times when you feel like you just need an infusion of green things, this is the meal you're looking for. The vegan "ranch" uses avocado for creaminess and arugula for a boost of vitamins and its emerald-green hue. For the vegetables, we use broccoli and small white turnips, often known as Tokyo turnips or Hakurei, which are popular at spring and fall farmers' markets. If you can't find the turnips, you can substitute 2 small Persian cucumbers for the turnip roots and 5 cups [75 g] baby kale for the greens.

FOR THE "RANCH" SAUCE

1 ripe Hass avocado

2 cups [40 g] arugula

2 Tbsp white miso

1 Tbsp fresh lemon juice

½ tsp Dijon mustard

¼ tsp garlic powder

Salt and freshly ground pepper

¼ cup [12 g] snipped chives

FOR THE BOWL

1 bunch small white turnips, with tops

Salt

½ tsp sugar

One 14 oz [400 g] package extra-firm tofu

1 medium to large stalk broccoli

Freshly ground pepper

4 Tbsp [60 ml] olive oil

2 garlic cloves, thinly sliced

1 cup [200 g] Jade Pearl Rice™ or short-grain rice, cooked (see page 48)

Furikake seasoning, for serving

TO MAKE THE SAUCE, in a blender, purée together the avocado flesh, arugula, 1 cup [240 ml] of water, the miso, lemon juice, mustard, and garlic powder until smooth. Taste and season with salt and pepper, if desired. Add the chives and pulse to incorporate.

TO MAKE THE BOWL, separate the tops from the turnips and roughly chop the leaves, stems and all. Clean by submerging in a large bowl of cold water and agitate to remove any grit.

Scrub the turnip roots, then slice about ¼ in [6 mm] thick. In a bowl, toss the turnips with ½ tsp of salt and the sugar and let stand while you prepare the rest of the dish, tossing the turnips occasionally.

Cut the tofu crosswise into 8 slabs. Dry them well between layers of paper towels.

CONT'D

Separate the stalk from the crown of the broccoli. Using a large knife, peel off the tough skin of the stalk. Cut the inner core of the broccoli into bite-size pieces. Pull apart the broccoli crown into small florets.

Season the tofu with salt and pepper. In a large skillet oil over medium-high heat, warm 2 Tbsp of the oil. Add the tofu slabs in a single layer and cook until well browned on the bottom, 3 to 5 minutes. Flip and cook until the other side is browned, 3 to 5 minutes longer. Transfer the tofu to a plate.

Add the remaining 2 Tbsp of oil and the broccoli, spreading it out in the skillet. Season with salt. Cook without moving for 1 minute, until starting to brown on the bottom. Stir the broccoli and cook until it's totally bright green, 1 to 2 minutes longer. Add the garlic and cook until starting to soften, 1 to 2 minutes. Lift the turnip greens out of the water and add them to the skillet. Stir and cook until the greens are wilted, about 2 minutes. Season with salt.

Spoon the rice into four bowls. Arrange two slabs of tofu in each bowl. Pile the cooked vegetables alongside. Drain any excess liquid from the turnips and divide them among the bowls. Spoon some of the avocado "ranch" over top, sprinkle the bowls with furikake seasoning, and serve, passing any remaining sauce at the table.

RICE BOWLS WITH PURÉED BLACK BEANS, CHILI SWEET POTATOES, AND LIME YOGURT

SERVES 4

While satisfying, sometimes rice bowls feel like they're merely a vehicle for cleaning out the fridge and need some help to make them a cohesive dish. Enter the purée. This one, made of black beans, really ties the dish together.

FOR THE ROASTED SWEET POTATOES	FOR THE BLACK BEAN PURÉE		FOR SERVING	CONT'D
2 large sweet potatoes, cut into ½ in [13 mm] pieces	1 Tbsp extra-virgin olive oil	One 14 oz [400 g] can black beans with their liquid, or 2 cups [320 g] cooked black beans plus ¼ cup [60 ml] water	½ cup [120 g] full-fat yogurt	
2 Tbsp extra-virgin olive oil	1 small yellow onion, chopped		Zest and juice of 1 lime	
1 tsp ground coriander	Salt and freshly ground pepper		Salt	
½ tsp ground cumin	1 garlic clove, thinly sliced		1 large or 3 small radishes, thinly sliced	
½ tsp ancho chile powder	½ tsp ground cumin		3 cups [360 g] warm cooked rice (see page 48)	
Salt and freshly ground pepper	¼ tsp ancho chile powder		1 ripe Hass avocado, diced	
			Cilantro leaves, for garnish	

TO MAKE THE ROASTED SWEET POTATOES, preheat the oven to 425°F [220°C].

Line a baking sheet with parchment paper, if desired. On the baking sheet, toss the sweet potatoes with the olive oil, coriander, cumin, and chile powder and season with salt and pepper. Roast for 20 to 25 minutes, until tender, stirring once halfway through.

TO MAKE THE BLACK BEAN PURÉE, in a saucepan or deep skillet over medium heat, warm the oil. Add the onion, season generously with salt and pepper, and cook, stirring occasionally until softened, about 5 minutes. Add the garlic and cook until fragrant, about 1 minute longer. Add the cumin and chile powder and cook just until fragrant, about 20 seconds. Add the beans with their liquid and cook, stirring, just to heat through to warm.

Scrape the bean mixture into a food processor and process to a slightly chunky, slightly loose purée, about 1 minute. Taste and season with more salt and pepper, if desired.

TO SERVE, in a small bowl, whisk together the yogurt with the lime zest and half the lime juice and season with salt.

In another small bowl, toss the radishes with the remaining lime juice and season with salt.

Season the warm rice with salt.

Spoon the black bean purée into bowls. Arrange the rice on top. Arrange the sweet potatoes, radishes, and avocado in piles around the bowl. Drizzle some of the lime yogurt on top, garnish with cilantro, and serve with the remaining lime yogurt at the table.

CHEESY RISOTTO-FILLED POBLANOS WITH PICKLED ONIONS

SERVES 4

Risotto might be an Italian dish, but it makes for a wonderful filling in these Southwest-inspired peppers. Tangy pickled onions keep the dish from feeling too rich. The recipe makes more onions than you'll likely need, so refrigerate the rest for up to 2 weeks to add to your tacos, sandwiches, and rice bowls.

FOR THE ONIONS

½ cup [120 ml] apple cider vinegar

2 tsp sugar

1 tsp salt

1 medium red onion, thinly sliced

FOR THE RISOTTO-STUFFED PEPPERS

4 very large poblano peppers or 8 medium poblano peppers

1 qt [960 ml] low-sodium chicken or vegetable broth plus 1 cup [240 ml] hot water, plus more water as needed

2 Tbsp extra-virgin olive oil

1 medium yellow onion, chopped

2 garlic cloves, thinly sliced

Salt and freshly ground pepper

2 Tbsp chopped fresh marjoram or oregano or ½ tsp dried oregano

1 cup [200 g] arborio rice

¼ cup [60 ml] dry white wine

6 oz [170 g] Monterey Jack cheese, grated

Roughly chopped cilantro, for serving

TO MAKE THE ONIONS, in a bowl, whisk together the vinegar, ½ cup [120 ml] of water, the sugar, and salt until the sugar and salt are dissolved. Add the onion and toss together. As you make the risotto, toss the onions every few minutes to help them absorb the pickling liquid.

TO MAKE THE RISOTTO-STUFFED PEPPERS, if you have a gas stove, roast the peppers directly over the gas flame, using tongs to turn them frequently and pressing to help the flame get into the crevices, until the skin is blackened all over, 6 to 10 minutes. If you do not have a gas stove, turn on the broiler. Broil the peppers as close to the heat source as you can, turning occasionally, until blackened all over, about 10 minutes. Transfer the blackened peppers to a bowl and cover with another bowl to allow them to steam while you make the risotto.

In a small saucepan, bring the broth and water to a simmer and keep warm.

CONT'D

In a heavy medium saucepan over medium heat, warm the olive oil. Add the onion and garlic, season with salt and pepper, and cook, stirring, until softened, about 8 minutes. Add the marjoram and cook until fragrant, about 30 seconds. Add the rice and cook for 1 minute. Add the white wine and cook, stirring, until nearly evaporated, about 1 minute. Add 1 cup [240 ml] of the hot broth and cook, stirring and occasionally scraping down the sides of the saucepan. When the liquid is nearly evaporated, add about ½ cup [120 ml] of the broth and cook, stirring, until nearly evaporated. Continue adding about ½ cup [120 ml] of the broth and cooking until nearly evaporated. After about 20 minutes, begin tasting the risotto, adding more liquid as necessary and cooking until the rice is al dente and suspended in a thick, creamy sauce; you may not use all the broth or you may need to add a little more liquid. Lower the heat to medium-low, add about 1 cup [about 100 g] of the cheese and stir until melted. Remove from the heat. Taste and season with more salt and pepper, if desired.

Preheat the oven to 350°F [180°C].

Uncover the peppers and use your hands to rub off as much of the blackened skin as possible. Use scissors to snip a T shape in the peppers so they are open from top to bottom with a horizontal slit at the top. Cut out the seeds from the inside of the pepper, removing as many seeds as possible.

Lightly oil a baking dish that's large enough to snugly hold the stuffed peppers. Arrange the peppers in the dish cut side up and season lightly with salt. Spoon the risotto into the peppers. Sprinkle the peppers with the remaining cheese.

Bake the peppers until the risotto is heated through and the cheese is melted, 10 to 15 minutes. Turn on the broiler to high and broil about 4 in [10 cm] from the heat source, turning the pan as necessary, until the cheese is starting to brown, 2 to 3 minutes. Let rest for 3 minutes, then sprinkle with cilantro and serve with the pickled onions.

PORTOBELLO RAMEN BURGERS

SERVES 2

The ramen burger is an internet phenomenon created by ramen lover and entrepreneur Keizo Shimamoto. Our rice ramen noodles work beautifully as the "bun" for these burgers, and we love to use one of the soup flavoring packets as the seasoning for the "burger," which in this case is a portobello mushroom.

To make the buns, you will need to mold the noodles into a nice round using 3 to 3½ in [7.5 to 9 cm] ring molds, ring caps from wide-mouthed canning jars, or cleaned tuna cans open on both ends. The sandwiches are admittedly messy, but they're also incredibly delicious and fun to eat.

2 portobello mushrooms	3 Tbsp canola oil
Two 2.8 oz [85 g] packages rice ramen, or other ramen with 1 soup seasoning packet	2 Tbsp mayonnaise
	Sriracha
	½ Hass avocado, thinly sliced, for serving
1 large egg, lightly beaten	Lettuce leaves, for serving
Salt	

Remove the stems from the portobello mushrooms if they have them and wipe the caps clean with a damp towel. Use a spoon to remove the gills, if desired.

In a large soup pot of boiling, well-salted water, cook the ramen noodles until just tender, about 4 minutes or according to the package directions. Drain well and run under water to help cool.

Set up a wire rack next to the stove.

In a large bowl, toss the ramen with the egg and ¼ teaspoon of salt.

In a large, well-seasoned cast-iron skillet or other heavy skillet over medium-high heat, warm 1 Tbsp of the oil until nearly shimmering. Arrange four ring molds in the skillet and divide the ramen mixture among them. (Alternatively, you can work in batches and cook 2 at a time.)

Season the tops with salt. Cook, pressing the noodles with a spatula once to even them out in the mold, until browned and set on the bottom, about 4 minutes. Carefully flip each ramen cake with the molds, season with salt, and cook until the bottom is browned and the noodles start to pull away from the molds, about 3 minutes. Transfer the noodle cakes to the wire rack and carefully pull away the molds, using a butter knife as necessary to loosen. If you have any stray noodles, you can trim the edges, if desired.

Wipe out the skillet and let the skillet cool to warm.

On a plate, brush the mushrooms with 1 Tbsp of the oil. In the skillet over medium heat, warm the remaining 1 Tbsp of oil until nearly shimmering.

Add the mushrooms to the skillet and cook, turning occasionally, until the mushrooms are nearly tender, about 3 minutes. Sprinkle the mushrooms with some of one of the soup seasoning packets and cook, turning occasionally, until tender, 2 to 3 minutes longer. Lower the heat if necessary if the spices are starting to burn. Transfer the mushrooms to the wire rack.

Meanwhile, in a small bowl, combine the mayonnaise with as much sriracha as you like.

Transfer 2 of the ramen rounds to plates. Arrange some of the avocado on top. Top with a mushroom, followed by the lettuce. Spread the mayo on one side of the remaining 2 ramen rounds, close the sandwiches, and serve.

ROASTED SQUASH WITH LEMONGRASS COCONUT CURRY BROTH AND BLACK RICE

SERVES 4

This fragrant yellow curry broth is inspired by the flavors of South India and Malaysia. It's mild enough for children to enjoy but you can make it spicy by serving it with sambal ulek. (The one from Brooklyn food company Auria's Malaysian Kitchen is especially good.) Here, the broth is served as a base for wedges of roasted squash to eat with a fork and knife, but it would be equally delicious with shrimp or chicken. Paired with the black rice, the dish is an elegant vegetarian main course.

1 medium winter squash (2 to 3 lb [910 g to 1.4 kg]), such as acorn or Robin's koginut, halved, seeded, and cut into at least 8 wedges

3 Tbsp melted coconut oil or canola oil

Salt and freshly ground pepper

2 lemongrass stalks

1 large shallot, roughly chopped

2 garlic cloves, smashed

Six ¼ in [6 mm] thick slices peeled ginger

2 tsp coriander seeds

½ tsp ground turmeric

Zest and juice of 2 limes

One 13½ oz [385 ml] can coconut milk

2 cups [480 ml] vegetable broth

1 cup [200 g] Forbidden Rice® or other non-sticky black rice, cooked and kept warm (see page 48)

1 cup [12 g] cilantro leaves, roughly chopped, for garnish

Sambal ulek, for serving

CONT'D

Preheat the oven to 425°F [220°C] and line a baking sheet with parchment paper.

Brush the squash wedges with 1½ Tbsp of the oil and season with salt and pepper. Roast the squash until browned on the bottom and tender within, about 35 minutes.

Chop off the top 4 in [10 cm] and the bottom of the lemongrass. Remove the tough outer pieces and save them to make tea or stock, if desired. Finely chop the tender inner core.

In a mortar or the bowl of a mini food processor, combine the lemongrass, shallot, garlic, ginger, coriander seeds, turmeric, a large pinch of salt, and ¼ tsp pepper. Add the lime zest and pound or pulse the ingredients together to form a paste.

In a medium saucepan over medium heat, warm the remaining 1½ Tbsp of the oil. Add the paste and cook, stirring frequently, until the paste no longer smells raw, about 2 minutes. Add the coconut milk and broth and bring to a boil. Lower the heat to medium-low and simmer just until the broth thickens and the flavors meld nicely, 5 to 10 minutes. Add the juice of one of the limes into the broth. Taste and add more juice from the second lime, if desired. Season the broth with salt and pepper.

Ladle the broth into bowls. Add wedges of squash and a scoop of black rice to each. Garnish with cilantro and pass sambal ulek at the table.

TOFU PULAO

SERVES 4

Our partner in India is Pratithi Organic Foods, founded by Tapan Ray. His wife, Paramita Ray, also a director in the company, provided this one-pot recipe, which she frequently cooks for her family using soy nuggets. (Here we use extra-firm tofu instead.) Tapan has been an important champion for organic rice production in India and has helped us source some of the most extraordinary-tasting Dehraduni basmati rice. Farmers he has trained to use SRI methods (see page 55) became the first rice farmers to qualify for Regenerative Organic Certification.

½ cup [120 g] full-fat yogurt

½ tsp turmeric

½ tsp mild chile powder, such as Kashmiri or ancho

Salt

8 oz [230 g] extra-firm tofu, diced into ½ in [13 mm] pieces

2 Tbsp ghee

¼ cup [60 ml] light olive oil or canola oil

1 medium yellow onion, chopped

2 oz [60 g] fresh ginger, peeled and finely grated

6 garlic cloves, finely grated

4 or 5 pods green cardamom, lightly smashed

2 whole cloves

1 whole star anise

2 bay leaves

1 Roma tomato, finely chopped

Freshly ground pepper

1 cup [200 g] white basmati rice, rinsed and soaked for 30 minutes, then drained well (see page 41)

4 or 5 cilantro sprigs, leaves and tender stems finely chopped, plus more for serving

10 mint leaves, torn, plus more for serving

CONT'D

In a bowl, whisk together the yogurt, turmeric, and chile powder and season generously with salt. Add the tofu and toss gently with the marinade to coat; let stand for 15 minutes.

In a large, heavy soup pot or Dutch oven with a tight-fitting lid over medium-high heat, melt the ghee in the olive oil. Add the onion, season generously with salt, and cook, stirring, until lightly browned, about 6 minutes. Add the ginger, garlic, cardamom, cloves, star anise, and bay leaves and cook until fragrant, about 1 minute. Add the tomato, season generously with salt and pepper, and cook, stirring, until softened, 3 to 4 minutes. Stir in the tofu with the marinade, then add the rice, cilantro, mint, 1¼ cup [300 ml] of water, and a few large pinches of salt. Bring to a boil, then lower the heat to medium-low, cover, and cook until the rice is tender, about 20 minutes. Turn off the heat and let stand for 5 minutes. Taste and season with salt.

Transfer the pulao to bowls, garnish with more cilantro and mint, and serve, being sure to avoid the whole spices as you eat.

BLACK RICE RISOTTO WITH DASHI, SCALLOPS, AND FURIKAKE BUTTER

SERVES 4

When we first started distributing our Forbidden Rice®, northern Italian cooking was all the rage, and a number of chefs made risotto with it. While it's not as starchy as Italian arborio and carnaroli rices, it does make a delicious risotto.

Instead of using a meat stock here, we opt for Japanese dashi—a simple, umami-rich stock often made with kombu (sea kelp) and smoked dried fish known as katsuobushi or bonito flakes. (There are other types of dashi you can try as well.) Both ingredients are available at many health food stores and well-stocked supermarkets, as well as Japanese markets, of course. Because dashi packs so much flavor with so few ingredients and so little time, you may find yourself making it regularly.

The risotto alone, perhaps with a sprinkle of green onions, is delicious. But the scallops and furikake butter make it special-occasion worthy.

FOR THE DASHI

1 oz [30 g] kombu (about 4 pieces)

1½ oz [45 g] katsuobushi flakes (also known as bonito flakes; about 3 cups)

FOR THE RISOTTO

1 leek

3 Tbsp unsalted butter

Salt

1 cup [200 g] Forbidden Rice® or other nonsticky black rice

¼ cup [60 ml] dry sake

1 Tbsp oil

1 lb [455 g] sea scallops, tough side muscle removed if needed

1 Tbsp furikake seasoning

Juice of ½ lemon

TO MAKE THE DASHI, in a large soup pot, combine the kombu and 2 qt [2 L] of water and bring to a bare simmer over medium heat. Lower the heat to medium-low and simmer gently (you do not want the kombu to boil) for 3 minutes. Using tongs, remove the kombu and reserve for another use (see Note).

Add the katsuobushi and simmer for 1 minute, then remove from the heat and let steep for 10 minutes. Strain the dashi, then return it to the pot and keep warm.

CONT'D

TO MAKE THE RISOTTO, trim off the roots of the leek and thinly slice crosswise into rings. As you reach the tougher dark-green parts, remove that layer and continue slicing the more tender light-green parts. (If you like, you can add the dark-green leek tops to the dashi to steep.) Transfer the leek to a bowl of water and swish to remove any grit, then drain.

In a heavy, medium saucepan over medium heat, melt 1 Tbsp of the butter. Add the leek, season with salt, and cook, stirring, until softened, about 3 minutes. Add the rice and cook, stirring, for 1 minute. Add the sake, increase the heat to medium-high, and cook, stirring, until evaporated, about 2 minutes.

Add 1½ cups [360 ml] of warm dashi to the rice and bring to a boil. Adjust the heat so the liquid is simmering around the edges of the pot and cook, stirring frequently, until most of the liquid is evaporated. Add just enough dashi to fully cover the rice and cook, stirring frequently—especially as more of the liquid evaporates—and occasionally scraping down the sides of the saucepan, until most of the liquid is evaporated. Continue adding liquid and cooking the rice this way until the rice is tender and suspended in a creamy-looking sauce, 40 to 50 minutes. (You may not use all the dashi, or you may need to add a little more water if it's not enough.) Season the risotto with salt.

When the rice is nearly cooked through, heat the oil in a large, heavy skillet over high heat until shimmering. Pat the scallops dry and season on one side with salt. Add the scallops, salted side down, and cook without moving until the sides start to turn opaque and the bottoms are deeply golden, about 2 minutes. Season the other sides of the scallops with salt. Using tongs, flip each scallop (if any are resisting, just let them cook a bit longer; they should release easily once browned). When all the scallops are flipped, turn off the heat and allow the residual heat to cook them so they are just barely opaque throughout, about 1 minute. Transfer to a plate. (Use a warm plate for extra credit.)

Add the remaining 2 Tbsp of butter to the skillet and let it melt over medium heat. When the foam subsides, add the furikake and cook until fragrant, about 15 seconds. Add the lemon juice to the skillet and remove from the heat.

Spoon the risotto into bowls and top with the scallops. Spoon the furikake butter over the top and serve.

NOTE

After you steep kombu for dashi, you don't need to send it right to the compost. Instead, you can make a sweet and savory kombu dish to serve alongside steamed rice. Just look up recipes for kombu tsukudani.

ONE-POT RED RICE WITH MUSSELS AND SWISS CHARD

SERVES 4

This one-pot dish is inspired by the American Southern dish known as perloo. The key to a good perloo is adding the ingredients in the right order so all are cooked properly. For this version, we parboil the red rice until it's tender because the tomato in the dish toughens the bran layer of the rice and slows down the cooking. We then steam mussels so they release their liquor and remove them so we can finish cooking the rice in their sweet, slightly briny broth. It's a little bit of fuss perhaps best reserved for weekend cooking, but it's well worth it.

1½ cups [300 g] red rice

1 bunch Swiss chard, stems separated from the leaves

2 lb [910 g] mussels, scrubbed and any beards removed

¼ cup [60 ml] extra-virgin olive oil

1 medium yellow onion, chopped

4 garlic cloves, thinly sliced

1 long red frying pepper, or ½ red bell pepper, finely chopped

¼ cup [3 g] parsley leaves, chopped

2 tsp fresh thyme leaves

1 tsp smoked paprika

½ tsp cayenne pepper (optional)

½ cup [120 ml] tomato passata (uncooked tomato purée)

Sliced green onions, for garnish

Fill a large soup pot with at least 12 cups [2.8 L] of generously salted water and bring to a boil over high heat. Add the red rice, lower the heat to medium, and simmer until tender, 30 to 35 minutes. Strain the rice, reserving the cooking liquid.

While the rice is cooking, finely chop the swiss chard stems. Separately, roughly chop the swiss chard leaves and set both the stems and leaves aside. Measure out 2 cups [480 ml] of the liquid and return it to the pot. Bring to a boil over medium-high heat, then add the mussels, cover, and cook for 2 minutes. Uncover, give the mussels a stir, and, using a slotted spoon, transfer any open mussels to a bowl. If not many mussels have opened, cover the pot for 1 minute, then uncover again. As the mussels open, use the slotted spoon to transfer them to the bowl and keep warm. Remove the pot from the heat. Discard any mussels that do not open.

CONT'D

Carefully tip any liquid in the bowl with the mussels into a measuring cup. Add the mussel-cooking liquid from the pot to the measuring cup until you have 2¼ cups [540 ml]. (Add water if necessary to equal that amount.)

In the same pot over medium heat, warm the olive oil. Add the onion, garlic, frying pepper, and chard stems. Cook, stirring occasionally, until the vegetables are softened, about 10 minutes. Add the parsley, thyme, paprika, and cayenne, if using, and cook until fragrant, about 1 minute. Add the tomato passata and cook, stirring, for 1 minute.

Add the parboiled rice and the 2¼ cups [540 ml] of the reserved liquid. Cover the pot and lower the heat to medium-low. Simmer for 15 minutes, then add the Swiss chard leaves to the pot, cover, and continue cooking until the leaves are wilted and the liquid is absorbed, about 10 minutes longer. Turn off the heat, return the mussels to the pot, and let stand for 5 minutes. Stir the rice and mussels together, then transfer to a large serving bowl, garnish with green onions, and serve.

QUICK-MARINATED SALMON WITH
COCONUT RICE, HERBS, AND FRIED SHALLOTS

**SERVES
4**

Inspired by the flavors of southern Vietnam, this is one of those dishes in which each component relies on the others and comes together to form a beautiful whole. For example, fried shallots serve as a garnish, and the flavorful oil they produce is used to season the rice and cook the fish.

For a lighter take on coconut rice, we use coconut water instead of milk because it lends a sweet nutty flavor without the richness.

Four 6 oz [170 g] salmon fillets (skin-on)

3 Tbsp fish sauce

2 Tbsp maple syrup

4 Tbsp [60 ml] unseasoned rice vinegar

1½ cups [360 g] jasmine rice, well rinsed and drained (see page 41)

2¼ cups [540 ml] coconut water, or 2 cups [480 ml] coconut milk plus ¼ cup [60 ml] water

Salt

¼ cup plus 2 Tbsp [90 g] canola oil

4 large shallots, thinly sliced

1 cup [40 g] finely chopped tender herbs, such as cilantro, mint, Thai basil, and dill

Chili-garlic sauce, for serving

Run your fingers along the salmon fillets to check for pin bones and remove if necessary.

In a shallow dish large enough to hold the salmon, whisk the fish sauce with the maple syrup and 2 Tbsp of the rice vinegar. Add the salmon and turn the fillets to coat. Let stand while you make the rest of the dish or for up to 1 hour.

In a medium saucepan, combine the rice with the coconut water and a couple of large pinches of salt; bring to a boil. Lower the heat to low, cover the pot, and cook until the rice is tender and the coconut water is absorbed, about 20 minutes. Turn off the heat and let stand for 5 minutes.

Meanwhile, set up a plate next to the stove lined with paper towels. In a large skillet over medium heat, warm about ¼ in [6 mm] of oil. When it shimmers, add the sliced shallots,

CONT'D

season with salt, and cook, stirring frequently, until they turn golden, about 6 minutes. (Keep a careful eye on them as you cook because they can go from golden to burnt quickly.) Working quickly, use a slotted spoon to transfer the shallots to the prepared plate. Season the shallots with salt. Remove the oil from the heat and let cool to warm, then strain the oil into a small bowl.

Add ¼ cup [60 ml] of the shallot oil and 1½ Tbsp of the rice vinegar to the warm rice. Season with more salt, if desired.

Preheat the broiler to high and line a baking sheet with foil. Remove the salmon fillets from the marinade and arrange them skin-side up on the baking sheet. Drizzle the skin with some of the shallot oil or plain canola oil and season lightly with salt. Broil the fish about 3 in [7.5 cm] from the heat source until the skin is nicely blistered and the flesh is just cooked through, 4 to 7 minutes, depending on the thickness of the fillets. Transfer to a plate or work surface and let cool slightly.

In a large bowl, toss the herbs with the remaining ½ Tbsp of rice vinegar. Add the rice to the herbs and stir to mix. Using a fork, flake the fish into large pieces, reserving the crispy skin, if desired.

At this point, you can either fold the fish into the rice before serving or spoon the rice into bowls and top with the fish. Just before serving, garnish the rice with the crispy shallots and salmon skin, if desired. Serve with chili-garlic sauce.

ARROZ CON POLLO

**SERVES
4 TO 6**

Someone could probably write an entire book about arroz con pollo (chicken with rice), a comfort food dish beloved throughout the Caribbean and Latin America. Some versions of this dish are a bit more complicated, relying on a slowly cooked and incredibly flavorful vegetable mixture known as sofrito. (Sofrito is a common flavor base for many dishes in Spain and Latin America, and if you have one already made, by all means, please use it.) Meanwhile, others are simpler and call for the vegetables to be cooked right in the pot as well as premade spice blends, including sazón and adobo seasoning.

For this one-pot version, we do make our own spice blend but cook the vegetables in the same pot as the chicken. A quick vinegar marinade on the chicken adds extra flavor and tenderizes the meat.

A drier-style long-grain rice works best for this dish; we use basmati. To brighten up the dish and add some crunch, you can serve the arroz con pollo with pickled onions (see page 173).

1 tsp ground cumin	1½ lb [680g] boneless, skinless chicken thighs	3 garlic cloves, finely chopped	1½ cups basmati [300 g] or other long-grain white rice, rinsed well and drained (see page 41)	½ cup [60 g] frozen peas
1 tsp paprika		¼ red, orange, or yellow bell pepper, finely chopped		⅓ cup [45 g] sliced green olives with pimentos
½ tsp ground coriander	2 tsp white distilled vinegar			
½ tsp dried oregano		Freshly ground pepper	2¼ cups [540 ml] chicken stock or water	Chopped fresh cilantro and and hot sauce, for serving
½ tsp garlic powder	¼ cup plus 2 Tbsp [90 ml] extra-virgin olive oil			
½ tsp turmeric		1 plum tomato, finely chopped		
Salt	1 small yellow onion, finely chopped			

In a small bowl, mix together the cumin, paprika, coriander, oregano, garlic powder, turmeric, and 1½ tsp of salt. In a large bowl, toss the chicken with the vinegar and add half the spice blend, rubbing it all over the chicken. Let stand for at least 20 minutes or refrigerate for up to 8 hours.

In a large Dutch oven or other heavy saucepan with a tight-fitting lid over medium heat, warm 2 Tbsp of the olive oil. Add the chicken and cook until golden brown on the bottom, 3 to 4 minutes. Flip and cook until golden brown on the other side, 3 to 4 minutes longer; adjust the heat as necessary to prevent the spices from burning. Transfer the chicken to a plate.

Add the remaining ¼ cup [60 ml] of the olive oil, then add the onion, garlic, and bell pepper, season generously with salt and pepper, and cook, scraping up any browned bits from the bottom of the pan, until very soft, about 10 minutes. Add the tomato and cook until softened, about 2 minutes. Add the remaining spice blend and cook until fragrant, about 1 minute.

Add the rice and several large pinches of salt and stir to coat the rice. Add the stock, increase the heat to medium-high, and bring to a boil. Lower the heat to medium-low, return the chicken to the pot, and cover with the lid. Cook until the rice is tender and absorbs the liquid, about 20 minutes. Turn off the heat, add the peas, and let stand for 5 minutes. Uncover, fluff the rice, and stir in the peas as well as the olives. Season with more salt and pepper if necessary. Sprinkle with cilantro and serve, passing hot sauce at the table.

COLD RAMEN WITH CHICKEN, EGG, SNAP PEAS, AND CARROTS

SERVES
4

This dish is inspired by hiyashi chūka, a chilled ramen dish that's popular in the summer in Japan. Some versions have the noodles swimming in a cool broth, while others, like this one, have a sauce that can be used for dipping or drizzling.

You can top cold ramen with almost any combination of vegetables and meat or fish that you like. This is just one suggestion.

FOR THE SAUCE

½ cup [120 ml] soy sauce

2 Tbsp sugar

2 Tbsp unseasoned rice vinegar

1 tsp finely grated fresh ginger (from 1 in [2.5 cm] peeled ginger)

1 tsp toasted sesame oil

FOR THE RAMEN

2 large eggs

Salt

10 oz [280 g] rice ramen noodles or other ramen noodles

4 oz [115 g] snap peas, trimmed and halved lengthwise

4 oz [115 g] carrots, cut into matchsticks

One 2 lb [910 g] rotisserie chicken, chilled, meat pulled

Thinly sliced green onion tops and toasted sesame seeds, for garnish

TO MAKE THE SAUCE, in a medium bowl, mix together the soy sauce, ¼ cup [60 ml] of water, the sugar, vinegar, ginger, and sesame oil.

TO MAKE THE RAMEN, bring a large soup pot of water to a boil over high heat and fill a bowl with ice water. Lower the heat to medium to maintain a simmer and carefully lower in the eggs. Cook the eggs for 7 minutes, then, using a slotted spoon, transfer to the bowl of ice water. When the eggs are cool, peel them and cut them in half lengthwise. Sprinkle with salt.

Return the water to a boil and season generously with salt. Add the noodles and cook until just tender, about 5 minutes or according to the package directions. Drain and rinse with cold water to cool.

TO SERVE, divide the noodles among four bowls. Arrange the snap peas, carrots, chicken, and eggs in the bowls and garnish with green onions and sesame seeds. Pour the sauce into four small bowls to serve alongside for dipping or spooning over the ramen.

CHICKEN JAMBALAYA WITH CHORIZO

SERVES 4

When you look at Louisiana jambalaya and at Spanish paella, you see echoes of each other. Both are rice dishes that start by sautéing aromatic vegetables. Both include sausage and either seafood or chicken or both. Both are wonderful ways to feed a crowd. Paella, which cooks uncovered in a wide pan, can take practice to get right. Jambalaya, however, is more forgiving.

This recipe brings together the aromatics of jambalaya—including the Cajun holy trinity of onion, celery, and green pepper—but calls for Spanish chorizo instead of the traditional andouille. For a Cajun-style jambalaya, this is on the milder side. If you like it spicier, add a bit more cayenne pepper or serve with hot sauce.

2 Tbsp extra-virgin olive oil

1 lb [455 g] boneless, skinless chicken thighs

Salt

4 oz [115 g] hard-cured sweet Spanish-style chorizo, halved lengthwise and sliced ¼ in [6 mm] thick

1 large yellow onion, chopped

1 green bell pepper, stemmed, seeded, and chopped

2 celery ribs, chopped

1 tsp garlic powder

1 tsp onion powder

1 tsp paprika

1 tsp dried thyme

½ tsp smoked paprika

¼ tsp cayenne pepper

¼ cup [60 ml] dry white wine

1½ cups [300 g] basmati or other long-grain white rice, well rinsed and drained (see page 41)

2¼ cups [540 ml] chicken stock or water

Chopped parsley and hot sauce, for serving

In a large, heavy soup pot or Dutch oven with a tight-fitting lid over medium-high heat, warm the olive oil until shimmering. Pat the chicken dry, season generously with salt, and cook without turning until well browned on the bottom, about 5 minutes. Lower the heat to medium, flip the chicken, and cook until browned and cooked through, about 5 minutes longer. Transfer to a cutting board and let cool.

Add the chorizo and cook just until the fat starts to render and the sausage pieces start to brown, 1 to 2 minutes. Using a slotted spoon, transfer to a bowl.

Add the onion, bell pepper, and celery to the pot, season with salt, and cook, stirring and scraping up any browned bits from the bottom of the pot, until very soft, about 10 minutes. Add the garlic powder, onion powder, paprika, thyme, smoked paprika, and cayenne and cook until fragrant, 15 seconds. Add the wine and cook, stirring and scraping up any more browned bits, until evaporated. Add the rice and a few pinches of salt, stir until coated, then add the chicken stock and bring to a boil.

Lower the heat to medium-low, cover, and cook until the rice is tender and the liquid is absorbed, about 20 minutes.

While the rice cooks, chop the chicken into bite-size pieces or use two forks to shred it.

When the rice is finished cooking, add the chicken and chorizo to the pot, cover, and let stand for 5 minutes. Stir to incorporate the chicken and chorizo into the rice. Transfer to bowls, sprinkle with parsley, and serve with hot sauce.

HAINANESE CHICKEN AND RICE

SERVES 4

Hainan is a small island off the coast of China, and versions of the chicken dish named for it are beloved in Southeast Asia, especially Singapore. To make it, you poach chicken to create a broth and then use the broth to cook the rice. Unlike you would with many broths, you do not want to strain the fat off this one because that fat helps create a gorgeously glossy rice. The flavor of this dish is all about the chicken, so use the best-quality bird you can.

Dipping sauces are also important and can vary quite a bit from cook to cook. Here, we suggest a simple green onion–ginger relish, a soy-based dipping sauce, and store-bought chili-garlic sauce.

FOR THE CHICKEN	FOR THE RICE	FOR THE SAUCES	
One 4 lb [1.8 kg] chicken	2 Tbsp canola oil	10 green onions, thinly sliced	2 Tbsp black vinegar or sherry vinegar
5 green onions, coarsely chopped	3 fat garlic cloves, finely grated	2 oz [60 g] fresh ginger, peeled and finely chopped	4 tsp brown sugar
1 oz [30 g] ginger, cut into coins	1 oz [30 g] fresh ginger, peeled and finely grated	3 Tbsp canola oil	Chili-garlic sauce or sambal ulek (optional)
8 garlic cloves, smashed and peeled	1½ cups [300 g] jasmine rice, rinsed and drained well (see page 41)	2 tsp toasted sesame oil	
Salt		Salt	
		¼ cup [60 ml] soy sauce	

TO MAKE THE CHICKEN, place the whole chicken in a large saucepan or stock pot. Add the green onions, ginger, and garlic. Fill the pot with water to cover the chicken by 1 in [2.5 cm], then add 1½ Tbsp salt.

Bring the water to a boil over high heat and skim any foam that rises to the surface. Lower the heat to medium-low and simmer, skimming any scum occasionally as necessary, until an instant-read thermometer reads 165°F [74°F] when inserted into the inner thigh of the chicken; this can take anywhere from 45 minutes to over 1 hour, so be sure to use a thermometer to check for doneness. Using tongs, carefully transfer the chicken to a carving board and let cool as you prepare the rest of the dish. Strain the broth and ladle out 2¼ cups [540 ml] of the chicken broth for the rice, being sure to include some of the chicken fat that rises to the surface of the broth. Reserve the remaining broth to drink with the meal or for another use.

TO MAKE THE RICE, in a small saucepan with a tight-fitting lid over medium heat, warm the oil. Add the garlic and ginger and cook, stirring, until no longer raw smelling, 1 to 2 minutes. Stir in the rice, then add the 2¼ cups [540 ml] reserved chicken broth and bring to a boil. Lower the heat to medium-low, cover, and simmer until the rice is cooked through and the liquid is absorbed, about 20 minutes. Turn off the heat and let stand for 5 minutes, then fluff with a fork or rice paddle.

TO MAKE THE SAUCES, in a medium bowl, toss together the green onions, ginger, canola oil, and sesame oil, then season with salt.

In another bowl, stir together the soy sauce, black vinegar, and brown sugar, mixing until the sugar dissolves.

TO SERVE, carve the chicken as desired and serve with the rice, sauces, and chili-garlic sauce, if using. You can also serve with some of the additional broth alongside.

SHIFTING TO ORGANIC
AND FAIR-TRADE AGRICULTURE:
A FARMING FAMILY'S STORY IN THAILAND

Fuangfah Punjit and her husband, Amporn Jaithong, are among the many rice farmers in Northeast Thailand (Isan) who supply certified organic and fair-trade jasmine rice to Lotus Foods. Their story is similar to that of many of the smallholder growers we work with who have found greater prosperity after switching from conventional to organic agriculture.

Currently, they farm 6 hectares (about 14 acres), on which they grow rice, fruits, vegetables, herbs, and spices. They have a son, a daughter, and two adopted younger daughters from a sister-in-law. The eldest two children completed vocational high school and found jobs away from the farm. However, their son, who studied electronics and was working in a cellphone repair shop, has returned to help his parents and may choose to make rice farming his livelihood.

Fuangfah and Amporn shared their thoughts about organic farming and fair trade: "We've seen that growing organic rice is better for our family because we have a better price," they said. "Plus we feel safer eating the rice that we grow.

"With fair trade and organic, we know in advance how much we will get paid for our paddy because there is the guaranteed buying price. Also, our costs are less because we use organic compost and organic fertilizer, which is much cheaper compared to the chemical fertilizer that we used before. After many years of using organic fertilizer, we can see that the soil quality gets better and now we can reduce that fertilizer quantity. Other than rice, we also grow organic chiles, shallots, and lemongrass. Before, we never thought of growing these products and only had income from selling rice. However, by recommendation from our organic rice mill, we did it and we can sell them at a good price as well."

Due to the increased income from their certified organic and fair-trade rice and vegetables, the two younger daughters

have the option to attend university. One of them would like to become a teacher of classic Thai performance. Perhaps even more heartening, Amporn doesn't have to leave his family anymore to do construction work in the city.

Regarding what they see as challenges to rice farming now and in the future, they said, "The climate is the main challenge. Rain and weather are impossible to control, and in the last couple of years, the weather has become unpredictable. We farmers do not know how to make it better and just have to live with it. Growing organic helps the soil to keep more moisture, but we still need rain first. We hope to have enough water for the growing season and hope that there will be no rain or too much fog at the time of harvest. There are not many prospects for young women in the province, but growing organic and fair-trade rice makes the prospects better for younger people to make a living as farmers."

ABOVE: Amporn Jaithong is on the left and Fuangfah Punjit is in the center.

THAI COCONUT RICE WITH
PAPAYA SALAD AND CHICKEN SKEWERS

SERVES 4

We work with a group of organic farmers in northern Thailand, and this recipe is inspired by the types of meals they cook at home. On the table, you'll often find an array of dishes, and the combination of salty, sweet, sour, and spicy flavors are a must at every meal. Coconut rice has a lightly sweet, buttery richness that's delicious with the fiery, tangy papaya salad and umami-rich charred chicken.

When making the salad, be sure to use a fully unripe papaya, which will be hard and green on the outside and rather neutral in flavor once peeled. If you can't find one, you can substitute shredded cabbage or kohlrabi for the papaya.

FOR THE CHICKEN	FOR THE RICE	FOR THE GREEN PAPAYA SALAD		CONT'D
2 garlic cloves, minced	One 13½ oz [385 ml] can coconut milk	½ small green papaya, peeled, seeded, and cut into large chunks	2 Tbsp fish sauce	
2 Tbsp fish sauce	1½ cups [300 g] white jasmine rice, rinsed (see page 41)		2 Tbsp fresh lime juice, plus more as needed	
2 Tbsp soy sauce		1 medium carrot		
1 lb [455 g] boneless, skinless chicken thighs or breasts, cut lengthwise into 1 in [2.5 cm] strips	1 Tbsp sugar	1 Tbsp small dried shrimp (optional, see Note)	1 tsp tamarind paste mixed with 1 Tbsp water	
	1 tsp salt	1 fat garlic clove, smashed	10 cherry tomatoes, halved	
		3 to 5 Thai chiles, thinly sliced	¼ cup [35 g] roasted peanuts, coarsely chopped	
		1½ Tbsp coconut palm sugar		

TO PREPARE THE CHICKEN, in a bowl or glass baking dish, whisk together the garlic, fish sauce, and soy sauce. Add the chicken, turn to coat, and refrigerate for 2 hours or up to 24 hours.

TO MAKE THE RICE, pour the coconut milk into a liquid measuring cup and add enough water to equal 2¼ cups [540 ml]. In a medium pot, combine the rice, coconut milk mixture, sugar, and salt and bring to a boil over medium-high heat, watching carefully so it doesn't boil over. Cover, lower the heat to medium-low, and cook until the rice is tender and the liquid is absorbed, 15 to 20 minutes. Turn off the heat and let stand for 5 minutes. (Because of the added sugar, you might get a little browning on the bottom of the pot, and that's okay. Add a little water to loosen it from the bottom of the pot and enjoy!)

TO MAKE THE GREEN PAPAYA SALAD, use the shredding blade of a food processor to shred the papaya and carrot.

In a mortar or mini food processor, combine the dried shrimp, if using, the garlic, chiles, and palm sugar and pound or pulse to form a coarse paste. Transfer to a large bowl. Add the fish sauce, lime juice, and tamarind paste mixture and taste to see if you like the balance; adjust as you like. Add the tomatoes, peanuts, papaya, and carrots and toss.

TO FINISH AND SERVE, preheat a grill or grill pan over medium-high heat for 10 minutes. If you're going to use wooden skewers, soak the skewers in water for at least 10 minutes.

Lightly oil the grates using an oiled paper towel. Thread the marinated chicken onto skewers and grill, turning frequently, until nicely browned and cooked through, 10 to 15 minutes. (If the chicken is sticking to the grates, allow it to cook another minute; it will release more easily as it browns.)

Serve the skewers with the coconut rice and papaya salad.

NOTE

Dried shrimp are used widely in East and Southeast Asian food. In northern Thailand, you find them frequently in papaya salads, either ground as they are here or left whole, so they get chewy in the dressing. You can find dried shrimp at many Asian markets or online. After opening the package, store them in the refrigerator.

VIETNAMESE PORK PATTIES WITH NOODLES AND DIPPING SAUCE

SERVES 4

This dish is inspired by the popular street food in Hanoi known as bún chả, in which deliciously flavored meatballs are grilled over charcoal and served in a cool sauce with noodles for dipping. This works best with thin rice noodles, such as rice vermicelli or the Lotus Foods Pho noodles.

FOR THE SAUCE

¼ cup plus 1 Tbsp [75 ml] unseasoned rice vinegar

¼ cup [60 ml] fish sauce

1 Tbsp brown sugar

1 garlic clove, thinly sliced

1 Thai chile, thinly sliced

FOR THE NOODLES AND MEAT PATTIES

1 lb [455 g] thin rice noodles, such as Lotus Foods Pho noodles or vermicelli

1 lemongrass stalk

2 garlic cloves, finely grated

1 large shallot, finely chopped

1 Tbsp finely grated fresh ginger (from 3 in [7.5 cm] peeled ginger)

2½ tsp fish sauce

2½ tsp brown sugar

1¼ tsp salt

¼ tsp freshly ground pepper

1½ lb [680 g] ground pork

FOR SERVING

Lettuce leaves

Sprigs of Thai basil, cilantro, and mint

Mung bean sprouts

Sriracha

TO MAKE THE SAUCE, in a medium bowl, whisk together 1½ cups [360 ml] of water with the vinegar, fish sauce, sugar, garlic, and chile and let stand while you prepare the rest of the meal.

TO MAKE THE NOODLES AND MEAT PATTIES, preheat a grill or grill pan over medium-high heat or set a broiler to high.

Bring a soup pot of water to a boil and set the noodles in a bowl. Pour the boiling water over the noodles and let stand for 4 minutes, then drain and rinse the noodles under cold water.

Chop off the top 4 in [10 cm] and the bottom of the lemongrass. Remove the tough outer pieces and save them to make tea or stock, if desired. Finely chop the tender inner core.

In a large bowl, stir together the lemongrass, garlic, shallot, ginger, fish sauce, sugar, salt, and pepper. Add the pork and use your hands to mix everything together until incorporated.

CONT'D

Form the meat into 16 small patties (each about 2 oz [60 g]). If you're going to use the broiler, line a baking sheet with foil. Set the prepared baking sheet under the broiler for 3 minutes until hot.

Arrange the meat patties on the grill, grill pan, or baking sheet and cook until nicely browned on one side, 4 to 5 minutes. Flip and cook until browned on the other side and cooked through, 3 to 4 minutes longer.

Transfer the patties to a plate and let cool for a few minutes.

TO SERVE, pour the sauce into four bowls and set them on four plates. If you like, you can add the meatballs right to the sauce. If the noodles are sticking together, rinse them again under cold water, then shake to drain; divide them among the plates. Arrange lettuce leaves, herbs, and mung bean sprouts on the plates alongside.

To eat, people can dip the noodles with herbs and sprouts into the sauce while breaking off pieces of the pork or they can create lettuce wraps with the meat patties and herbs, then dip the noodles in the remaining sauce. Serve with sriracha.

SHRIMP PASTE FRIED RICE WITH SWEET PORK

SERVES 4

Khao kluk kapi, or shrimp paste fried rice, is another favorite dish of the rice growers in northern Thailand. Typically, the rice is served in the center of a table alongside a few different accompaniments, like caramelized pork belly, egg ribbons, and juicy raw fruits and vegetables.

Shrimp paste, also known as belacan, is a hard brown paste made from salt and fermented shrimp; it's a popular ingredient in Southeast Asian and southern Chinese cooking. It's salty and funky but mellows when cooked, much like anchovies. You can find it at Asian markets or online; opt for Thai shrimp paste if you can.

FOR THE PORK BELLY	FOR THE OMELET	FOR THE SHRIMP FRIED RICE	FOR SERVING
1 Tbsp canola oil	2 large eggs	2 Tbsp canola oil	Sliced mango
1 large shallot, finely chopped	Salt	2 garlic cloves, finely grated	Sliced cucumber
One 1 lb [455 g] piece of pork belly, cut into ½ in [2.5 cm] pieces	1 Tbsp canola oil	2 to 3 tsp shrimp paste	Sliced chiles
½ cup [80 g] coconut sugar		3 cups [360 g] cooked and cooled jasmine rice (see page 48), preferably day-old	Lime wedges
3 Tbsp fish sauce			
2 Tbsp soy sauce			

TO MAKE THE PORK BELLY, in a deep skillet over medium heat, warm the oil. Add the shallot and cook until translucent, about 3 minutes. Stir in the pork, sugar, fish sauce, and soy sauce followed by just enough water to cover the pork when it's arranged in a single layer. Increase the heat to medium-high, bring to a boil, then lower the heat to medium-low to maintain a simmer. Cover and cook, stirring occasionally, until the pork is tender, about 1 hour. Using a slotted spoon, transfer the pork to a bowl. Increase the heat to high and cook the sauce, stirring occasionally, until it is thickened and glossy, about 10 minutes. Return the pork to the sauce, stir to coat, and keep warm.

MEANWHILE, TO MAKE THE OMELET, in a small bowl, beat the eggs and season with a large pinch of salt. In a small nonstick skillet over medium heat, warm just enough oil to coat the bottom of the skillet. Add the eggs and swirl the pan to form a thin, even layer. Cook the eggs until the bottom is set, about 2 minutes. Carefully flip the omelet and cook until set, about 30 seconds longer. (If it tears, that's okay.) Transfer the omelet to a cutting board and let cool slightly. Roll the omelet into a cylinder and slice into ribbons.

TO MAKE THE SHRIMP FRIED RICE, in a medium skillet over medium heat, warm the oil, then add the garlic. Cook, stirring, until fragrant, about 20 seconds. Add 2 tsp of the shrimp paste and use a spoon to break it up into the oil, about 20 seconds. Increase the heat to high, add the rice, and cook, pressing the rice to break up any clumps and stirring to incorporate the shrimp paste. Taste the rice and add more shrimp paste if desired, remembering the pork will be quite flavorful and salty as well.

Serve the shrimp fried rice with the pork, egg ribbons, mango, cucumber, chiles, and lime.

SPICY NOODLES WITH BOK CHOY AND PORK OR TOFU

SERVES 4 TO 6

This quick noodle dish gets its sweet, umami-rich heat from gochujang, a Korean red chile paste made with sticky rice powder and fermented soybeans. You can make the dish with ground pork or, for a vegetarian version, silken tofu. If you use tofu, add more toasted sesame oil at the end for richness, plus a bit more soy sauce to season.

¼ cup [60 ml] soy sauce

1 Tbsp sherry vinegar

1 Tbsp dark brown sugar

4 garlic cloves, finely grated

1 Tbsp finely grated fresh ginger (from 3 in [7.5 cm] peeled ginger)

1 tsp toasted sesame oil

1 tsp gochujang, plus more for seasoning

¼ tsp smoked paprika

1 lb [455 g] Lotus Foods Pad Thai noodles or other medium-thick rice noodles

2 Tbsp canola oil

1 lb [455 g] ground pork or one 14 oz [400 g] package silken tofu, drained

1 lb [455 g] baby bok choy, trimmed, washed well, leaves left whole and separated

Salt

Thinly sliced green onions, for garnish

In a small bowl, combine the soy sauce, vinegar, and sugar and whisk to dissolve the sugar. Whisk in the garlic, ginger, sesame oil, gochujang, and smoked paprika.

In a large pot of boiling water, cook the noodles until just cooked, 5 minutes. Drain and rinse.

Meanwhile, in a large skillet over medium heat, warm the canola oil. Add the pork or tofu, season lightly with salt, and cook, breaking it up with a spoon. (Be gentle with the tofu, if using.) Cook the pork until brown in spots and nearly cooked through, 5 minutes. (Cook the tofu just until warm, 2 minutes.) Add the sauce and cook, scraping up any browned bits from the bottom of the pan, until slightly thickened, 2 minutes. Add the bok choy, toss, and cook until wilted, about 1 minute. Rinse the noodles once more and add them to the skillet. Cook and toss until coated with the sauce and warmed through, about 1 minute, seasoning with more soy sauce, gochujang, or salt, if desired.

Serve the noodles in bowls and garnish with green onions.

BROWN RICE PILAF WITH CUMIN LAMB, KALE, AND SALTED YOGURT

SERVES 4

This one-pot dish, inspired by flavors of the eastern Mediterranean, is satisfying and grounding. If you enjoy a little fruit with your lamb, dried currants would be a lovely addition. Fresh mint, raw cucumber, and yogurt brighten it up.

4 Tbsp [60 ml] extra-virgin olive oil

1 lb [455 g] ground lamb

Salt

3 garlic cloves, finely chopped

2 tsp ground cumin

½ tsp ground turmeric

¼ tsp freshly ground pepper, plus more for seasoning

1 large red onion, chopped

1½ cups [300 g] brown basmati or other brown long-grain rice

2⅔ cups [640 ml] low-sodium chicken or vegetable broth

1 small bunch kale, stems and tough ribs removed, leaves thinly sliced

1 cup [240 g] full-fat Greek yogurt

Fresh mint and sliced cucumber, for serving

In a large, heavy pot with a tight-fitting lid over medium-high heat, warm 2 Tbsp of the oil. Add the lamb, season with salt, and cook, stirring to break it up into small pieces, until cooked through, 6 minutes. Add the garlic and cook, stirring, until fragrant, 1 minute. Add the cumin, turmeric, and pepper, and cook until fragrant, 1 minute. Using a slotted spoon, transfer the lamb to a bowl.

Lower the heat to medium and warm the remaining 2 Tbsp of oil (or use the fat remaining in the pan). Add the onion, season generously with salt, and cook, scraping up any browned bits from the bottom of the pan, until softened, 5 minutes. Add the rice, broth, and a large pinch of salt, increase the heat to medium-high, and bring to a boil. Lower the heat to medium-low, cover, and simmer until the rice is tender and the liquid is absorbed, 35 minutes.

Turn off the heat, add the lamb and kale, and let the pilaf stand until the kale is wilted, 5 minutes.

In a small bowl, season the yogurt with salt. Fluff the pilaf and serve with fresh mint, sliced cucumber, and the yogurt.

BURMESE-INSPIRED NOODLES WITH SAUSAGE AND SPICED TOMATO SAUCE

SERVES 4

Burmese Shan noodles—typically made with pork or chicken in a spiced tomato sauce—are pure comfort food. The dish comes from Burma's eastern Shan state, but it's a popular dish in other parts of the country and at American Burmese restaurants.

Using sweet Italian sausage is not traditional, of course, but hear us out: The spices in this sausage typically include fennel, garlic, and paprika—all spices in Shan noodles, so the flavors are just amplified. Plus, you can opt for sausage made from any meat you choose, or go for a vegetarian version.

Some versions of the dish are served with pickled mustard greens as a topping. Here, we add quick-marinated or tender mustard greens, which are a tasty addition but far less pungent. If you have pickled mustard greens, serve them alongside instead.

3 Tbsp canola oil

¾ lb [340 g] tender Asian mustard greens, roughly chopped

Salt

1 Tbsp white distilled vinegar or cider vinegar

1 large yellow onion, chopped

4 garlic cloves, thinly sliced

2 tsp finely grated fresh ginger (from 2 in [5 cm] peeled ginger)

1 lb [455 g] loose sweet Italian sausage (squeeze sausage from their casings if necessary)

½ tsp five spice powder

½ tsp paprika

¼ tsp ground turmeric

One 14½ oz [415 g] can whole tomatoes with liquid

1 Tbsp soy sauce

1 lb [455 g] Lotus Foods Pad Thai noodles or other medium-thick rice noodles

Chopped roasted peanuts, for serving (optional)

CONT'D

Bring a large soup pot of generously salted water to a boil.

In a wok or deep, wide skillet over medium-high heat, warm 1 Tbsp of the oil until shimmering. Add the tender mustard greens and stir-fry until starting to soften, 30 seconds to 1 minute. Transfer the greens to a bowl. Season generously with salt and toss with the vinegar.

Wipe out the wok or skillet, then warm the remaining 2 Tbsp of oil over medium-high heat. Add the onion, season generously with salt, and cook, stirring frequently, until softened, about 5 minutes. Add the garlic and cook, stirring frequently, until softened, about 2 minutes. Add the ginger and cook, stirring frequently, until no longer raw smelling, about 1 minute. Add the sausage and, using a spoon, break it up into chunks—the smaller the better. After it's broken up, stir and cook to coat with the aromatics. Increase the heat to high and cook without stirring for 30 seconds to 1 minute to allow the sausage to brown in spots, then stir and repeat the process until the sausage is cooked through and lightly browned.

Lower the heat to medium and add the five spice powder, paprika, and turmeric and cook, stirring, until incorporated and fragrant, about 15 seconds. Add the tomatoes and their liquid and the soy sauce and bring to a boil. Stir to scrape up any browned bits on the bottom and sides of the pan. Lower the heat to medium-low and simmer, stirring occasionally and using your spoon to break up the tomatoes as they soften, until the sauce is slightly thickened and glossy, about 15 minutes.

Meanwhile, add the noodles to the boiling water and cook, using tongs to move them around and keep them separate, until just tender, about 5 minutes. Drain.

When the noodles and sauce are ready, run warm water over the noodles to help stop them from sticking, then taste. Season them with salt, if desired.

To serve traditionally, divide the noodles among four bowls and serve the sauce on top. Sprinkle with roasted peanuts, if using, and serve the greens alongside. Alternatively, toss the noodles with the sauce in the wok, then top with the peanuts and serve with the bok choy.

5

DESSERTS

THE FUTURE OF RICE

It's hard to believe that such a small, unassuming grain is pivotal to dealing with some of this century's most pressing challenges, including climate change, water availability, loss of biodiversity, food security, and even migration.

By 2050, our planet will have welcomed 2 billion more people than live on it today. That's just around the corner! We have about 25 years to figure out how to ensure that they will have access to nourishing food. Most of the increase in our planet's population will occur in regions where rice is grown, so it's alarming when experts warn that by 2025, some 17 million hectares [65,000 square miles]—about twice the area of South Carolina—of flooded rice fields in Asia will be experiencing water scarcity. Already in some parts of Pakistan, farmers are prohibited from growing rice due to water shortages. There is real urgency in getting "more crop from every drop."

Some farmers are transitioning to growing more drought-tolerant crops such as millet, sorghum, and fonio, and that trend should continue. When farmers became able to irrigate their fields, rice often displaced these nutritious, traditional staples. However, as more people join the world and transition to plant-based diets, the popularity of the much-beloved rice will continue to increase, and we need to figure out how to grow it in a way that benefits the planet and its people.

As we make changes, we must do so in a way that acknowledges the vital contributions of farmers. They are stewards of large swaths of our planet's land and thus custodians of unique species of plants and animals as well as inherited wisdom, languages, cultures, and traditions. Their work benefits us all.

The good news is that rice production can be regenerative and profitable for smallholder farmers, enhancing yields of both traditional and modern varieties, with more efficient and beneficial use of land and water resources and less emission of greenhouse gases. The System of Rice Intensification (SRI, see page 55), has been effective in all major rice-growing ecosystems around the world and can boost the yields of other major cereals and food crops as well.

Project Drawdown, an organization devoted to reducing worldwide production of greenhouse gases as quickly and efficiently as possible, identified SRI as one of the top one hundred solutions currently available that, if scaled up, could help the planet reverse global warming while swelling rice supplies and enhancing farmers' livelihoods. Presently, only about 10 percent of rice farmers are using some or all of the SRI practices. To scale up SRI and other water-saving rice production strategies will require interventions by governments and the private sector.

However, as consumers, we also have a critical role to play. Our lives are greatly enriched by the delicious, colorful, and diverse bounty from farmers' fields. Our purchasing choices send strong messages to policymakers, farmers, and companies about how much we value this biodiversity and that it be produced in eco-friendly ways. Consumers are already emerging as a force for driving positive change. As we have long said, we can all be part of the solution to make the world a better place. So, let's get going and "Do the Rice Thing!"

HORCHATA MILKSHAKES

SERVES 4

Horchata is a cool, creamy drink originally from Valencia, Spain, that is now popular throughout Latin America. In Spain, it's typically made with tiger nuts, but in Latin America, it's often made with rice and sometimes almonds. Here, we blend horchata into a thick milkshake for a special dessert treat. A high-speed blender works best for making the horchata, if you have one.

1 cup [200 g] white rice

1½ cups [360 ml] whole milk

¼ cup [35 g] roasted almonds

1½ qt [780 g] vanilla ice cream

½ tsp cinnamon, plus more for sprinkling

In a bowl, combine the rice, milk, and almonds, and refrigerate for 8 to 12 hours.

Let the ice cream stand at room temperature for 10 minutes to soften. Meanwhile, transfer the rice mixture to a blender and blend on high speed for 1 minute until puréed. Line a fine-mesh sieve with 2 layers of cheesecloth and strain the purée into a bowl. Rinse out the blender.

Return the strained horchata to the blender and add the ice cream and cinnamon. Blend, starting on low speed and working your way up to medium speed, until the milkshake is pourable; scrape the sides or use a blender plunger as needed. Pour into glasses, sprinkle with cinnamon, and serve.

CHAMOMILE RICE PUDDING WITH STRAWBERRIES

SERVES 4

Chamomile's gentle sweetness is just right with rice, and it tastes especially gorgeous with strawberries. This pudding calls for arborio rice; while it takes a bit longer to cook, it does have a wonderful creamy texture. The recipe here makes a looser rice pudding. If you like a thicker style, reduce the amount of liquid you add or cook it a bit longer until it thickens.

FOR THE RICE PUDDING

5 cups [1.2 L] milk

5 chamomile tea bags or 5 tsp dried chamomile

½ cup [100 g] arborio rice

½ cup [100 g] sugar

¼ tsp salt

FOR THE STRAWBERRIES

1 pint [340 g] strawberries, hulled and sliced

¼ cup [50 g] sugar

Pinch of salt

TO MAKE THE RICE PUDDING, in a medium saucepan over medium heat, bring the milk just barely to a boil. Add the tea bags, then turn off the heat. Let steep for 10 minutes, then remove the bags or strain off the loose tea. Ladle out 1 cup [240 ml] of the milk and let cool.

Add the rice, sugar, and salt to the pot with the milk and bring to a simmer over medium heat. Cook, stirring occasionally, being sure to scrape the bottom of the pot, until the rice is tender and the pudding is a bit soupy, about 40 minutes. Remove from the heat and let stand for 30 minutes. If the pudding is seized and very thick, stir in some of the reserved milk until you like the consistency.

MEANWHILE, TO PREPARE THE STRAWBERRIES, in a skillet over medium-low heat, toss together the strawberries, sugar, and salt and cook until the sugar is melted and the juices start to thicken but the strawberries retain their shape, about 3 minutes. Let cool.

Transfer the rice pudding to glasses and top with the strawberries and some of their liquid. Chill until cold, at least 2 hours. Serve cold.

CHOCOLATE-COCONUT RICE PUDDING

SERVES 4 TO 6

In this "I can't believe it's vegan" pudding, rice gets cooked in luscious cocoa-infused coconut milk. While you can leave the pudding chunky, like a typical rice pudding, you can also blend it to create a rich, smooth pudding with a fun, stretchy texture. (A high-speed blender works best.) By sprinkling almonds on top, you give the whole dessert an Almond Joy vibe.

½ cup [100 g] white short-grain rice

Two 13½ oz [385 ml] cans coconut milk

½ cup [100 g] sugar

3 Tbsp cocoa powder

1 tsp vanilla extract

¼ tsp salt

Smoked or salted roasted almonds, roughly chopped, for garnish (optional)

In a saucepan over medium heat, combine the rice, coconut milk, sugar, cocoa powder, vanilla, and salt and bring to a simmer, stirring to dissolve the sugar and cocoa powder. (Don't worry if the cocoa powder is a little lumpy; it will incorporate as it cooks.) Cook, stirring occasionally and scraping the bottom and sides of the saucepan to prevent scorching, until the rice is tender and the pudding is starting to thicken but still a bit soupy, about 30 minutes. At this point, you can serve the pudding warm or chill before serving.

If you would like a smooth pudding, let cool until just warm, then transfer to a blender. Purée on high speed for about 1 minute, stopping to scrape the sides of the blender as necessary. Transfer to an airtight container and refrigerate until well chilled. (You can press plastic wrap on the surface of the pudding to prevent a skin from forming.) If you would like to loosen the pudding at all, whisk in a little milk of your choice.

Sprinkle the pudding with almonds before serving, if using.

MAKE AHEAD The pudding can be refrigerated in an airtight container for up to 4 days.

A GARDEN OF EDEN IN INDIA

Indian conservationist and activist Sabarmatee and her late father, Radha Mohan, are living proof that we can grow rice using an agro-ecological approach while stewarding the land in a way that promotes biodiversity. Thirty years ago, they purchased a barren piece of land in Odisha, a state on India's northern Bay of Bengal coast, with the goal of rejuvenating it through organic farming. Local farmers and other experts discouraged them; the inland parcel suffered from deforestation and erosion as well as abuse from pesticides and fertilizers. Undeterred, they set up a nonprofit called Sambhav, which means "possible," and got to work. First, they widely planted leguminous crops because they fix nitrogen in the soil to help rebuild it. As the soil healed, they allowed many "weeds," including bamboo and other grasses, to thrive when they popped up voluntarily. They also mulched and mulched and mulched, which gave cover to ants and other insects that acted as helpers by creating tunnels to aerate the soil. Plus, as the mulching material breaks down, it feeds the soil and slowly brings it back to life. After several years, the soil became fertile enough to grow fruit trees, many of which were planted by birds naturally through their waste.

Along with the site's managed forestland filled with fruit trees, Sabarmatee cultivates about five hundred varieties of rice using the System of Rice Intensification (see page 55), as well as about one hundred different varieties of vegetables and legumes on a few acres of land. To continue growing rice as dry spells become longer, she created an elaborate system of three ponds to capture the rainwater, with the one at the highest elevation feeding the one at the bottom. The water from the bottom pond flows gently like a spring into the rice paddy fields, allowing her to keep the soil damp using conserved water even when there's a drought.

The site, which now totals ninety acres, has become a veritable Garden of Eden, with over a thousand species of plants thriving there with

countless insects, birds, and animals. Sambhav also serves as a regenerative agriculture training resource and seed exchange. Growers from all over India visit the site, and while they're there, Sabarmatee shares seeds with all who want them. In exchange for the seeds, she asks them to take an oath that they will steward them for as long as they can. Many of the indigenous rice varieties she shares produce high yields even in challenging conditions, from steep elevations to the high winds and drought that have become more normal with climate change. She often advises farmers to grow a few different varieties, so if one is knocked down by wind or overtaken by a plant disease, there are others that will produce a healthy crop. When growers have success with the indigenous varieties they get from Sabarmatee, neighboring farmers then plant them. The result: Households that are more food secure in the face of climate change and less reliant on outside companies for their seeds.

To help support Sabarmatee's work, we've sponsored her participation in the International Rice Congress to share her research about the System of Rice Intensification and the effect on women's lives. In 2018, she received India's highest civilian award for women's empowerment, called the Nari Shakti Puraskar. She remains an inspiration for us every day at Lotus Foods, and we're thrilled to share her story more widely.

KHEER

SERVES 4 TO 6

Rice kheer (also known as payasa in Bengal or payasam in Southern India) is an ancient and popular dessert in the Indian subcontinent. It is a dish you might frequently find cooked in homes or at Hindu temples. This recipe comes from Munny Yadav, an organic rice farmer in Kalayakhera Village in Uttar Pradesh in northern India. "Kheer as a dessert after lunch acts as a nourishing tonic and gives people an overall feeling of satisfaction," she says. We couldn't agree more.

¾ cup [150 g] white basmati rice, rinsed (see page 41)

1 qt [960 ml] whole milk

4 strands saffron

1 Tbsp ghee

½ cup [70 g] raw cashews

6 Tbsp [75 g] sugar

½ tsp ground cardamom

2 Tbsp sliced toasted almonds or chopped shelled roasted salted pistachios

1 to 2 Tbsp raisins

In a medium bowl, cover the rice with water and soak for 20 minutes. Drain well.

In a saucepan over medium heat, bring the milk to a simmer. Transfer ¼ cup [60 ml] of the warm milk to a small bowl and add the saffron. Keep the milk warm.

In medium, heavy saucepan over medium heat, melt the ghee. Add the cashews and toast, stirring, until fragrant and browned in spots, 3 to 4 minutes. Transfer the cashews to a cutting board and let cool, then coarsely chop.

Add the rice to the saucepan and stir to coat with any remaining fat. Carefully pour in the warm milk and bring to a simmer. Cook the rice, stirring occasionally, until tender, about 20 minutes. Stir in the sugar and cook, stirring frequently, until the kheer is thick, about 10 minutes more. Remove the kheer from the heat and stir in the saffron threads with the milk and the cardamom as well as most of the cashews, almonds, and raisins. Serve warm or chill and serve cold, topping with the remaining cashews, almonds, and raisins. You can add more milk as needed to loosen.

FINNISH-INSPIRED RICE PASTRIES

MAKES 16 PASTRIES

In Finland, people make savory pastries known as Karjalan pies using a rye crust and simple rice filling. Inspired by those, we created a lightly sweet version that is tasty for breakfast or dessert, perhaps with some fresh fruit. As a sweet surprise, spread 1 tsp of jam on the bottom of each pastry before adding the rice.

FOR THE FILLING

1 cup [200 g] white short-grain rice

1½ cups [360 ml] whole milk

⅓ cup [65 g] sugar

1 tsp vanilla extract

¼ tsp salt

FOR THE CRUST

1 cup [110 g] dark rye flour

¼ cup plus 1 Tbsp [45 g] all-purpose flour, plus more for dusting

½ tsp fine salt

4 Tbsp [60 g] butter, melted

TO MAKE THE FILLING, in a medium saucepan over high heat, combine 2 cups [480 ml] of water with the rice and bring to a boil. Lower the heat to medium-low, cover, and cook until tender, about 20 minutes. Add the milk, sugar, vanilla, and salt, then increase the heat to medium-high and cook until a pudding forms, about 5 minutes. Let cool to room temperature.

TO MAKE THE CRUST, preheat the oven to 450°F [230°C] and line two baking sheets with parchment paper.

In a large bowl, whisk together the flours with the salt. Add almost ½ cup [120 ml] of water and stir until a stiff dough forms, adding more water if needed to bring it all together. The dough will be a little bit sticky but still stiff.

On a floured work surface, shape the dough into a log and cut into 16 equal-size pieces, forming each into a round. Using a floured rolling pin, roll out each round into a 4 to 5 in [10 to 12 cm] circle, flouring the work surface as needed. Spoon 2 to 3 Tbsp of the rice pudding into the center of the pastry, leaving a ½ in [13 mm] border. Fold up the edges around the filling, forming it into a small, oval-shaped tart. Crimp the edges, then transfer to the prepared baking sheet. Repeat with the remaining pastries.

Brush the pastries with melted butter and bake for about 10 minutes, until the dough is set and the edges are lightly browned. Let the pastries cool on the baking sheet and serve.

RICE PUDDING CHEESECAKE
WITH ALMOND CRUST

**SERVES
8**

Now you no longer need to choose between these two creamy desserts! With rice serving as a thickener rather than eggs, you don't have to bake the filling and risk a split cheesecake.

To make the cake, you'll need an 8 or 9 in [20 or 23 cm] springform pan, which allows you to unmold the cake easily. An 8 in [20 cm] pan creates thicker layers of crust and filling.

FOR THE CRUST

½ cup [70 g]
rice flour

¼ cup plus
2 Tbsp [45 g]
almond flour
or almond meal

¼ cup [50 g]
packed brown
sugar

¼ tsp fine
salt

4 Tbsp [55 g]
butter, melted

FOR THE FILLING

1 qt [960 ml]
whole milk

1 cup [200 g]
white short-
grain rice

½ cup [100 g]
sugar

½ tsp fine
salt

8 oz [230 g]
cream cheese,
cut into
8 pieces

1 tsp vanilla
extract

Cinnamon, for
sprinkling

TO MAKE THE CRUST, preheat the oven to 350°F [180°C]. Line the bottom of an 8 or 9 in [20 or 23 cm] springform pan with parchment paper.

In a bowl, whisk the flours with the sugar and salt. Add the butter and stir until incorporated. Press into the bottom of the prepared pan and bake until the crust is dry, 20 minutes.

TO MAKE THE FILLING, in a medium saucepan over high heat, combine the milk, rice, sugar, and salt and bring to a boil. Lower the heat to medium and simmer until the rice is tender and the pudding starts to thicken, 20 minutes. Add the cream cheese and stir until melted, then remove from the heat. Stir in the vanilla extract and let the mixture cool to warm, stirring occasionally, 20 minutes.

Spread the filling over the crust and refrigerate until chilled, 4 hours. Run a butter knife around the edge of the cake, then remove the springform to unmold. Dust the cake with cinnamon. Cut into slices and serve.

MATCHA RICE PUDDING

SERVES 6

In Japan, the green tea powder known as matcha is a frequent addition to desserts, and it's a natural match for anything creamy. To keep the texture of the pudding loose, we find it's best to add the last bit of liquid after the rice has cooked and cooled a bit. To further highlight the green color of the tea, we use our Jade Pearl Rice™ here, but white short-grain rice works just as well. If you'd like to make a vegan version of the dish, use canned coconut milk.

1 cup [200 g] Jade Pearl Rice™ or white short-grain rice

½ cup [100 g] sugar

½ tsp salt

6 cups [1.4 L] whole milk

4 tsp matcha tea powder

In a large saucepan over medium-high heat, combine the rice, sugar, salt, and 5 cups [1.2 L] of the milk until it just barely boils. Stir frequently, scraping the bottom of the pan. Lower the heat to medium-low and simmer, stirring occasionally, until the rice is very tender and the pudding is thickened but still a bit soupy, 18 to 20 minutes. Remove the pudding from the heat and let stand until it's just above room temperature (about 30 minutes). It will thicken significantly as it stands.

Meanwhile, in a small bowl, vigorously whisk the remaining 1 cup [240 ml] of milk with the matcha and let stand for at least 5 minutes. Whisk once more to make sure it's nicely combined, then fold it into the rice pudding.

Serve the pudding at room temperature or lightly chill for about 2 hours before serving. The pudding will continue to thicken as it stands or chills.

AFTERWORD

So, what will it take to scale up innovations like System of Rice Intensification (SRI, see page 55) that can reduce and even reverse the warming of our planet, while also positively benefiting global farming communities and food security?

Perhaps most important, we need to change our mindsets when it comes to agriculture. At present, governments, international donor organizations, and corporations focus on applying more external inputs like new seeds and fertilizers and extracting greater yields. Conventional high-input methods could ramp up yields, but only with ever-increasing quantities of seed, water, and agrochemicals derived from fossil fuels. This approach is not only costly for farmers, but it comes at the expense of human and ecosystem health. It has also led to greater concentrations of land and supply-chain ownership, including consolidated control over seeds and inputs.

Agriculture, and especially rice farming, must be reframed. No other human activity has more direct impact on achieving so many of the UN's Sustainable Development Goals. Building resilient rural communities with improved nutrition, enhanced social status for farmers, and sustainable use of land and water requires a more holistic agro-ecological approach.

The most expensive investment for governments will be to improve irrigation infrastructure and management so that the smaller, intermittent quantities of water needed for SRI and other water-conserving approaches can be delivered reliably. (As water becomes scarcer and more valuable, the profitability of these investments will only increase.)

The private sector can make modest but essential investments that can have major impacts by training farmers, especially women, to grow rice using SRI and other agro-ecological practices, designing and manufacturing affordable, small-scale equipment suitable for women as well as men, providing crop insurance and price incentives for farmers who adopt regenerative practices, building community mills and storage facilities to reduce post-harvest losses, and supporting farmer-owned cooperatives.

Smaller community-owned mills promote greater equity in rural communities because they help keep supplies under local control. Local mills also allow producers to retain broken grains, bran for livestock feed, and husks for fertilizer or fuel—all valuable byproducts that are lost to them when their rice is processed by large, centralized mills.

Technology has a role to play, too. Smartphones and online platforms can facilitate farmers' access to markets with better information about prices, credit, and buyers. Hopefully, these technologies will enable farmers using regenerative practices to enhance their incomes through participation in carbon-trading programs.

When customers like you advocate for these kinds of policies and investments, we believe it will be possible to stimulate rural employment and innovation, attract young people to careers in agriculture, inject more food into local markets, boost farmers' livelihoods, and contribute to the goal of carbon neutrality by 2050.

In addition to supporting better rice production with your purchasing decisions, you can also give back to or get involved with the organizations on the following pages.

ORGANIZATIONS TO SUPPORT

JUBILEE JUSTICE

This nonprofit works to restore and accelerate Black land ownership and stewardship and support Black farming communities through new models of regenerative farming. One of its first major initiatives is to provide capital financing to Black farmers growing SRI rice in the United States. Lotus Foods has partnered with this nonprofit to act as a guaranteed buyer of the rice. *jubileejustice.org*

REGENERATIVE ORGANIC ALLIANCE

Regenerative agriculture is one potential solution to the climate crisis. This organization certifies farmers who practice regenerative agriculture and educates farmers in how to incorporate regenerative methods. *regenorganic.org*

SRI GLOBAL

This nonprofit organization promotes the System of Rice Intensification (SRI) to benefit rice farmers in developing countries. *facebook.com/ SRIGlobal*

PROJECT DRAWDOWN

As we mentioned on page 218, Project Drawdown has identified SRI as one of the top one hundred solutions currently available that, if scaled up, could help the planet reverse global warming while helping farmers. Donate to help its mission of reducing greenhouse gases and the effects on our planet quickly, safely, and equitably. *drawdown.org*

ONE STEP CLOSER

If you are a business owner or CEO, consider joining this organization, which is devoted to tackling the major environmental issues that affect us today. *osc2.org*

ACKNOWLEDGMENTS

This cookbook, as with almost all projects we've embarked on for the last twenty-five plus years, has been a collective effort. Many individuals have brought their talents, interests, and energy to create something much more wonderful than what we initially thought possible.

We are so grateful to our agent, Leigh Eisenman, for seeing the potential for this book and guiding us through the process to get here—thank you!

It has been an exceptional experience to collaborate with Kristin Donnelly, whose creativity and global thinking has resulted in such fun, delicious, and innovative recipes.

And thank you to Nicole Perry, who tested every single recipe in this book and was never afraid to give pointed feedback. The recipes are even better because of her work. Thank you as well to Sara Maniez for your last-minute testing.

Warm thanks to our editor at Chronicle Books, Deanne Katz, for helping us make this book better than we could imagine. And thank you to Leigh Saffold, who shepherded the manuscript through the initial and final rounds of edits.

Thank you to the rest of the team at Chronicle: Magnolia Molcan, Margo Winton Parodi, Lizzie Vaughan, Tera Killip, Steve Kim, Cynthia Shannon, Keely Thomas-Menter, Mikayla Butchart, and our sensitivity readers.

To Erin Scott, who photographed all the recipes, and, along with Lillian Kang's master styling, did a magnificent job of making them and our rice come to life and look extra delicious! We are so grateful for the amazing work of the rest of the photography team—Paige Arnett, Huxly McCorkle, and Eliza Miller.

Our profound and immense gratitude to Olivia Vent, who in 2005 introduced us to the System of Rice Intensification and became an integral part of both our journey and this cookbook.

We would further like to express our sincerest appreciation to our colleagues Sue Price and Erika Styger, who generously made available their photographs, taken while documenting the lives and work of rice farmers in Asia, Africa, and Latin America.

And none of this would have been possible without our wonderful Lotus Foods team, who work tirelessly every day to bring about the change we seek.

We are grateful for the love and support from our families. A special thank-you to Wah Chung Lee, Ken's dad, whose culinary mentoring was as much about how to interact with people as it was about harmonizing food ingredients in making a great fried rice!

We extend a huge thanks to our remarkable supply partners around the world who are as passionate as we are about improving farmers' lives and changing how rice is grown to be more sustainable and equitable.

Finally, we continue to be inspired and motivated by the knowledge, skill, and hard work of the thousands of family farmers we work with who each year harvest some of the finest rice in the world, to share with us and you.

ABOUT THE CONTRIBUTORS

Caryl Levine and Ken Lee are co-founders and co-CEOs of Lotus Foods, Inc., the successful organic and specialty rice company based in the San Francisco Bay Area. Husband and wife, Ken and Caryl started Lotus Foods in 1993, pioneering the introduction of heirloom red and black rice to US markets, starting with Bhutanese red rice and a black rice they trademarked as Forbidden Rice®. Together they have reshaped how Americans think about and eat rice.

Both are passionate about empowering women farmers, creating a more equitable food system, and ensuring consumers have healthier rice options. Their work has received abundant recognition. The Specialty Foods Association honored Ken and Caryl each with a Leadership Award, for Citizenship and Vision, respectively. In 2017 *Conscious Company Media* selected Ken and Caryl to receive their first-ever Leadership for Global Impact Award, recognizing leaders "using the power of business as a force for positive change." In 2021 Caryl was among the Real Leaders 100 Women in Impact, which recognized one hundred women who are "leading the way towards a brighter future."

Kristin Donnelly is the author of *Modern Potluck* and *Cauliflower* from Short Stack Editions as well as the co-author of *The Chef's Garden* by Farmer Lee Jones. She loves nothing more than being part of the cookbook-writing process. You can find her at kristindonnelly.com or in her kitchen in New Hope, Pennsylvania, where she lives with her husband, daughter, and rescue pup.

BOTTOM LEFT: Lotus Foods co-founders and co-CEOs Caryl Levine and Ken Lee (middle) with a group of SRI farmers in Cambodia.

ABOUT LOTUS FOODS

Lotus Foods, Inc. is one of the most successful organic and specialty rice companies in the United States. As a Certified B Corp™, Lotus Foods is committed to using business for the benefit of people and the planet. They introduced a new paradigm using market incentives for social change and paying farmers premium prices to conserve rice biodiversity, improve incomes, protect the environment, and provide consumers with healthier rice. From their grassroots beginnings, they now import specialty rice and value-added products from a global supply chain and distribute it to thousands of outlets throughout North America. Since the company's founding, their products have won sixteen sofi™ awards from the Specialty Foods Association, as well as many NEXTY awards from New Hope Natural Foods, sponsor of the Natural Products Expo (East and West), two industry organizations devoted to high-quality foods. Their most recent award was sofi™ Gold for their Dehraduni basmati rice from northern India, which is also the first rice to receive a Regenerative Organic Certification (ROC) by the Regenerative Organic Alliance. The company and its products have been featured in newspapers across the country, including the *New York Times*, *San Francisco Chronicle*, *Washington Post*, *Wall Street Journal*, and many food magazines, including *Food & Wine*, *Eating Well*, and *Bon Appetit*.

INDEX